MORGAN

D0348354

COVENTRY LIBRARIES & INFORMATION SERVICES

WITHDRAWN

FOR SALE

3 8002 02422 725 0

CHARLOTTE BROWNE

ULTIMATE FOOTBALL HEROES

MORGAN

FROM THE PLAYGROUND TO THE PITCH

DINO

Coventry City Council	
ALD	
3 8002 02422 725 0	
Askews & Holts	May-2019
	£5.99

First published in paperback in 2019

ISBN: 978 1 78946 108 4

All rights reserved. No part of this publication may be reproduced, stored in a retrieval system, or transmitted in any form or by any means, without the prior permission in writing of the publisher, nor be otherwise circulated in any form of binding or cover other than that in which it is published and without a similar condition including this condition being imposed on the subsequent purchaser.

British Library Cataloguing-in-Publication Data:

A catalogue record for this book is available from the British Library.

Design by www.envydesign.co.uk

Printed and bound in Great Britain by Clays Ltd, Elcograf S.p.A.

1 3 5 7 9 10 8 6 4 2

© Text copyright Charlotte Browne 2019

The right of Charlotte Browne to be identified as the author of this work has been asserted by her in accordance with the Copyright, Designs and Patents Act 1988.

Every reasonable effort has been made to trace copyright-holders of material reproduced in this book, but if any have been inadvertently overlooked the publishers would be glad to hear from them.

John Blake Publishing is an imprint of Bonnier Books UK
www.bonnierbooks.co.uk

To George and Rob for their kindness,
support and laughs aplenty.

ULTIMATE
FOOTBALL HEROES

Charlotte Browne knew from a young age she would probably
end up working with words. She has worked as a journalist for a
number of publications, from *The Independent* to *Prima*, and written
for organisations within the not-for-profit and charity sectors.
She is probably at her happiest walking in the Cornish countryside,
swimming in the sea or playing her favourite songs on piano.
She lives in south London.

Cover illustration by Dan Leydon.
To learn more about Dan visit danleydon.com
To purchase his artwork visit etsy.com/shop/footynews
Or just follow him on Twitter @danleydon

CONTENTS

CHAPTER 1

WHICH SPORT?

Jenny and Jeri Morgan both gazed proudly down into the cot, staring at the peaceful face of the sleeping baby.

'Welcome your new baby sister to the world,' said their mother Pamela.

'She's so beautiful, Mom,' said Jenny.

Jeri looked up at her father Michael. 'She's so cute!' she said. 'But it's just too bad you didn't get a boy. That's what you wanted, right?'

Michael laughed. 'It doesn't quite work like that, Jeri!'

'So you won't send her back, Dad? Mom?'

They both looked at Jeri and smiled.

'No way!' replied Michael. 'She's perfect.'

'Our little Alexandra,' said Pamela.

'Alex... an... dra.' At four years old, Jeri struggled a little to pronounce the name.

'You can say Alex too,' said Pamela.

'I'm glad you're not sad, Dad,' said Jeri. 'I want us to keep her.'

'Hey,' said Michael, 'we're delighted. I promise I'll only ever send her back if she's not a baseball fan!'

They all laughed. 'That would be impossible in this family!' said Pamela.

'And in this state!' said Michael. 'Home of the Angels – the best baseball team in Los Angeles!'

*

Alex beamed as she felt the wind in her hair and heard her dad shouting from the sidelines: 'Go Ali Cat!!!'

It was a typically warm Californian day at her school and she'd just taken off from the starting line, in a race to support a local homeless charity in Diamond Bar. She was running against the fastest boys in her class at Maple Hill elementary school.

But she wasn't fazed for a second. She'd already earned the nickname 'Mighty Mouse' at the age of five, because when she ran she went so fast her chest puffed out. She knew she could beat them, just as she beat them at tetherball, one of her favourite games.

'Keep your eye on the finishing line,' she told herself, 'run it three seconds faster this time, three seconds.'

Alex was always setting goals for herself and although she knew she could outrun her opponents, she always wanted to beat her personal best. She was used to her older sisters being better, faster and stronger. So she always strove to keep up with them. Above all this though, she loved the feeling of running, feeling the world whizz past as she accelerated, and the joy of speeding past the other runners as they struggled to keep up with her.

'Yay!' she threw her hands up in the air as she crossed the finishing line and heard the crowd cheer. She was sure she'd beaten her previous time.

But if there was anything she loved better than running, it was running after a ball. She'd recently joined the AYSO (American Youth Soccer Organization) and enjoyed it immediately for the chances it gave her to run around the field and play on mixed teams, where she regularly outplayed the boys too.

Her speed amazed the coaches and the parents in the crowd.

'Michael, she's just so fast – it's incredible!'

'I know,' he nodded proudly. 'But you should see her catch, she's brilliant at that too.'

He added: 'Since I first taught her at three, her skill was obvious then.'

'Well I dunno Michael, I think she's gonna want to stretch those legs.'

Michael laughed. 'Oh, she's very athletic, she can play volleyball and soccer really well. But she's destined for baseball. I just know it.'

*

It was a Saturday and Alex and her sisters, plus dad Michael, were all off to an Anaheim Angels baseball game, one of the biggest teams in the American league. Alex was dressed in her green Oakland

Athletics T-shirt and shorts with matching cap.

Baseball was Michael's favourite sport (along with the rest of America) and he encouraged all of his three daughters to build their skills and excel at the game, coaching them in a team called the A's.

Alex always loved the atmosphere in the stadium and knew how much the game meant to her sisters and her dad. For years, she'd gone to watch them play in their leagues and though she admired how good her sisters were, she got a little fed up with always being seen as the baby and 'Jeri's little sister', always one step behind them in strength and skill. She just wanted to be Alex, in her own right.

When she protested, her mother would say: 'But you're the baby, Alex, our little Ali Cat, of course you're not going to be as strong as them, and that's okay.'

Michael, who loved to encourage healthy competition in every game – not just baseball, but from Monopoly to cards – would chuckle at this and say:

'Ali Cat – don't forget the glove now!'

'No, Dad!'

'You never know when you might catch a foul ball! You've got to show your sisters how good you are!'

'I am as good as them,' she thought to herself defiantly. 'And there's one thing I'm definitely better at.'

Before they got in the car to leave, Alex turned to her sister.

'Hey Jeri – let's race! To the bottom of the road!'

Jeri sighed as they stood at a makeshift starting line, ready to take off.

'Alex, come on now. You're like nine. *I'm* thirteen. You've got no chance.'

'Just you watch me!'

'Fine! I'm not going easy on you – no head starts!'

Their dad shouted from the car: 'On your marks, get set... go!'

Alex sped off down the road as Jeri flailed behind her, easily crossing the finishing line way before her. Jeri finally caught up, out of breath and spluttering. Alex did a little dance for joy in a circle.

'Told you! Told you!'

CHAPTER 2

DIAMOND HEIGHTS

'Aaww!' Pamela smiled as she spotted a note left for her on the fridge. Her girls often left surprise messages for her around the house. Both Michael and Pamela encouraged them to think about and write their different goals down on a regular basis, however big or small, whether they were school or sport-related.

Pamela recognised this particular note as one of Alex's straight away, from her handwriting and the dozens of hearts. It said: 'Hi Mommy! My name is Alex and I am going to be a professional athlete for soccer! I <3 you always, Ali Cat.'

Pamela beamed as she looked outside at the yard and saw Alex practising keepie-uppies with her football. She'd known for a while it was her daughter's favourite sport. She couldn't mistake the joy on her face when she saw her sprinting about on the pitch, always racing after the ball and on the attack. Yes, Alex was an all-round athlete and brilliant at baseball, but she was clearly more in her element when running and chasing.

She went outside and called to Alex. 'Hey honey! Thank you for your letter!'

Alex waved back to her. Pamela walked over to her daughter. 'Ali, I'm really pleased you know what you want to do so early and we'll support you, every step of the way.'

'Thanks, Mom.'

She winked. 'Just let your dad know, okay?'

Alex's face fell. This was something she'd been dreading a little. She'd grown bored of baseball, but knew how much her dad loved the sport and wanted her to pursue it fully. After dinner that evening, Alex looked across the table at him, and decided to bite the bullet. There was no easy way to say it, so better to be honest and straight.

'Dad.'

'Yes, sweetie?'

'You know what?' She took a deep breath. 'I don't like baseball.'

'What?' She saw the shock on his face. 'But you're so good.'

'I like soccer. I like to run.'

His face softened. 'Yeah, I can see that. I'm sorry. Maybe I've pushed baseball too much.'

'No, Dad – it's okay! I just, really love football! It's my sport!'

He smiled. 'I know, I know. Well, if you're going to be a professional footballer I guess we'd better get started on making sure that really happens! You're going to need a coach!'

Alex felt a weight lift from her shoulders as she ran round the table to hug him. 'Thank you, Dad! Thank you!'

*

Alex couldn't help but smile. Her dad had never really seen the appeal of football but ever since she'd admitted it was what she wanted to truly focus on, he'd taken lessons in coaching and was taking more interest in the technique involved in the game. He'd bought a pop-up goal for them to practise with, sometimes up to four or five times a week. They'd go across to the street to middle school, or Pantera Park if there were people on the field. Her dad always made sure they found somewhere.

'Okay, Alex,' said her dad. 'Making a shot is one thing. But actually *finishing* – now that's a whole different ball game. Where do you want the ball to go? High or low in the goal? You've got to know where you want to go!'

'Dad, can we do finishing tomorrow? I'm tired.'

'Al, there is always someone out there who's prepared to work harder than you. And you want to be the best, right?'

Alex nodded.

'Then let's keep going. And I promise, you'll have your favourite ice cream from 7-Eleven if you finish at least three out of five goals where you want them.'

'Okay, Dad!'

As a warm-up he also encouraged Alex to practise running laps with ankle weights.

'Dad – what are you trying to do to me?!'

'It'll help your endurance, Alex. And boy – will you feel the difference when we take them off!'

It was true – without weights she felt as though she was flying when she ran. Her dad was pushing her but it felt so good to have him as a coach, someone who took her seriously. And even better, he was now coaching her AYSO soccer team Diamond Heights who he'd led through the Championship League.

Alex knew that the extra training with her dad had helped improve her confidence on the pitch, especially when it came to finishing the goals. She was beginning to feel less like shy little Alex, who walked in the shadows of her big sisters. She'd been one of their top scorers and she didn't want to disappoint the team in the final against the CDA Slammers. They were a tough team, known for their experienced goalie.

'You can do this, Alex,' said her dad, 'you're getting better all the time.'

Alex was learning that one of her main skills was keeping the pressure on in attack. She never let up and was always looking for opportunities to get on the ball, even when the other players were flagging a little.

At half-time her mum brought down orange and strawberry slices for the team.

'This will keep you all going!'

'Thanks, Mrs Morgan!' they all chimed in unison. They all loved Alex's mum – not only she did bring them treats but she also made hair ties for each player, with their uniform number glitter-glued on.

'Go get 'em, team!'

Sixty minutes into the game and the Slammers had just levelled. None of them wanted a tie that would take them into extra time. Alex could sense the team were relying on her and it was down to her to shake things up a little. She made contact with the ball in midfield and dribbled down the right wing, using her preferred strong left leg. There was a defender hot on her heels but Alex was just too fast. All those practice sessions dribbling at speed with her dad were paying off. A space opened up for her and she sensed the goalie was taken aback by her pace.

'Don't look them in the eyes!' her dad always told her.

'Where do you want it to go?' she heard him ask in her head.

'Low!' she replied as she booted it into the net.

GOAL!!!

She swelled with pride as she heard the recognisable sound of her mum and sisters cheering above the crowd – 'Go Ali Cat!! Go!'

The team worked hard to hold off the Slammers' attackers until the whistle blew.

'You go, guys – high fives all round!' Alex's mum ran on to the pitch to congratulate them all with flowers. Alex had achieved one of her first soccer goals – she'd won a Championship League tournament.

CHAPTER 3

TEENAGE DREAMS

It was the summer of 1999 and Alex couldn't take her eyes off the TV screen. The USA team were playing China in the final of the Women's World Cup at the Rose Bowl in Pasadena, all of thirty miles away from Diamond Bar. Alex was devastated not to have tickets to the event and she couldn't believe there was a soul in the crowd more excited than her. As she watched the match, she clutched her dad's arm intensely and gasped every time she caught sight of the 90,000 spectators in the stadium – it was the highest attendance any women's sporting event had ever seen, with good reason.

It had been an incredible tournament with Mia

Hamm, Julie Foudy and Brandi Chastain displaying such extraordinary skill that the entire country had fallen in love with them. Each player had taken the women's game to a new level and proven the high standard that the sport could achieve. They'd become idols all over the country for many young girls – especially one player.

'Dad – look! There she is!' Alex squealed with delight as Kristine Lilly bounded on to the pitch in her Number 13 shirt, with a huge infectious smile on her face.

'That's who I want to be!' cried Alex. It was true. Kristine was the kind of forward player that Alex dreamed of becoming, not least for her speed. 'I want to play that position!'

'Yeah,' said her dad, 'she's got a real energy about her. She's a game changer alright.' He turned to Alex as he said: 'And I bet she's worked hard to be there.'

She didn't take her eyes off the screen for a second throughout the game, not even to pick up the popcorn they'd stockpiled in front of them for the night.

'You can miss so much – even in a second!' she
thought. She felt as though she would explode
with tension as the game went to a penalty shoot-
out. When Brandi Chastain booted in the final
kick Alex and her entire family whooped and jumped
up and down for joy. They felt as though they were
celebrating with the entire country in their living
room.

That night Alex lay awake, too excited to sleep.
She knew exactly the path she wanted to take in
life. 'That is going to be me someday,' she said to her
teddy bear. 'When I grow up, I am going to play in
the World Cup final. And I am going to win.' Deep
down she knew this to be true.

*

'Aw, you AYSO players, you always seem to think
you can just waltz in and play club soccer straight
away!'

Alex stared up at the coach, feeling as though
she'd been punched in the stomach. He looked
down at her, with a hint of amusement and ridicule
in his eyes.

been told she wasn't good enough. In the American
Youth Soccer Organization she was used to being
the best in pretty much every team she'd ever
played on. At the age of thirteen, it was clear she
was getting so good that she needed to progress
an environment where the sport was taken mo
seriously. She practised every day but knew s
to take the next step towards her dream of pl
professionally. That next step was club socce
was picked in tryouts she could play teams a
state, not just in her town. And most import
all, colleges recruited out of club teams and
whether a player deserved a scholarship.

'Hey,' the coach continued, 'you've no
on the team but we're putting you in as
player.'

A practice player? Alex wasn't even

she said to herself as she ran out to start warming up,
'give them a big smile, be confident.'

She ran over to the team where they were
ctising drills, put on a brave face and said 'Hello!'
ightly as she could. No-one responded. A couple
d round, stared blankly in her direction, and then
ued to ignore her. Alex suddenly longed for
O teammates, her real friends. She thought of
playing together, not taking it all so seriously,
ng fun. She knew they'd be missing her.

walked away, she heard one of the girls
d caught the tail-end of some mean chat:
ie practice team.' Then: 'No way will she
nd 'She's joined too late, who does she

s it,' she vowed to herself. 'I'm
going to prove the coach and my

teammates wrong. I'm going to go to practice every day and get better.'

She kept this promise, practising as hard as she could, every single day, for a place on the team. But still, the coach didn't put her in.

'Don't get disheartened, Alex,' her dad said, 'you are good enough. More than good enough.'

'I dunno, Dad, maybe I started too late – a lot of the girls there have been playing club soccer since they were eight or nine.'

'Honey, I think that would have been too much pressure too early. I'm glad you had that fun time playing. You'll get there at your own pace, I just know it.'

After three months, though, Alex was beginning to feel miserable and she'd still not forged any close friendships. She felt isolated and alone.

'Okay,' agreed her dad, as he realised how sad she was. 'Let's just try another club.'

'Really?'

'Sure, this club obviously isn't right for you. What about Cypress Elite?'

'But Dad, they're in Orange County, that's a lot further away for practices. At least half an hour by car.'

'That's okay, we can help you. I know how committed you are.'

'Oh Dad, thank you!'

'Thank me when you've got on the team!'

CHAPTER 4

A SERIOUS COMPETITOR

The sun beat down in Cypress, California. Alex ran out onto the field for her first day of practice with Cypress Elite in their purple-and-white kit. She was overjoyed to have made it on to their team but she knew there was a lot of work ahead of her. However, one of the first activities their coach Dave Sabet asked them to do was one of her all-time favourites.

'Okay guys, I'd like you to sprint down the field...' He'd barely finished the sentence when Alex took off, leaving a trail of club players struggling to keep up behind her.

Dave took her aside after practice. 'Wow. Alex, so how do you think today went?'

Alex blushed a little. 'Er, pretty good, I think.'

'You have phenomenal speed. Clearly.'

'Thanks.'

'But your technical skills – we've really got to work to catch up on those. Soccer takes more than speed. It takes craft. Precision.'

'I'll put the work in! I want to learn. That's why I'm here.'

'Okay, I can see that. But there are gaps in your basic skills. Are you prepared to come earlier and stay later to do some extra training with us?'

'Yes – anything! I really want to play better.'

'Okay, excellent! Then we can't wait to get working with you!'

For the next six months Dave, and his two assistants Sal and Eduardo, gave Alex extra support and training. In particular they worked on improving her shots and passes, and helped her to analyse the game.

'It's all in the details, Alex – get those perfected, then you can just keep building upon those skills.'

Her parents were extremely pleased to see how much happier Alex was.

'It feels great to have a coach who believes in me, Dad,' she told Michael.

'Yes, we can both see the difference that's made,' he replied. 'And all this hard work you've put in – it's going to pay off.'

The hard work paid off quicker than Alex was expecting. Within six months she was called up to the Cal South ODP (Olympic Development Program), which identified players showing promise for the national team.

'Dad, it's the same program that's trained Landon Donovan who plays for Galaxy! And Joy Fawcett – legend!'

Her dad beamed with pride. 'You're a serious competitor now, Alex. I think it's time we took you shopping.'

'What?'

'Come on, let's go.'

Alex grinned from ear to ear as her dad took her to the shoe department at the back of the sporting goods department. Her mouth dropped open as he found a salesperson and said: 'Can you bring us the very best cleats that you have?'

'Dad? What?'

She looked down at the boots the salesman brought. The price tag on them was $320.

Alex wasn't sure what to say. She thought of all the things her dad could buy for himself with that money. She froze there for a second, her eyes fixated on the tag.

'Well, what are you waiting for, try them on,' her dad said.

Tentatively, Alex tried them on. They fitted and cushioned her feet perfectly.

'Dad, I love them. But... they cost sooooooo much money.'

He smiled and said: 'Let's get 'em!'

*

Alex sped down the pitch towards the ball, racing ahead of her San Diego opponent. It was the second half of the final of the Cal South Cup Under 16s Championships. Cypress had a clear 2–1 lead. Alex caught up with the ball and deftly shot it across to her teammate Sandy down the right wing.

She caught it on first touch and slammed it into the net.

GOAL!!!

It wasn't long until the whistle blew and the team ran towards each other to hug and celebrate. As they lifted the Cal South Cup high, Alex realised how much she was learning at Cypress.

She thought back to how she played on the AYSO teams. Back then, she probably wouldn't have assisted on the final goal, she would rather have taken the shot herself, to take all the personal glory. But here, as she learnt and developed new playing techniques, she understood that, ultimately, it took teamwork to win a game.

As she looked around at her smiling, happy teammates, she knew that none of them could win alone. She was finally part of a team that trusted and relied on each other and she knew this would one day take her through to success at the highest levels.

CHAPTER 5

ANYTHING CAN HAPPEN
IN A MINUTE

Although it was winter, the Californian sun was still
shining brightly. Alex was at the Home Depot Center,
looking forward to a friendly game against the men's
junior national team. She'd started playing with
the women's U-17 national team since the youth
national coaches had discovered her through the
Olympic program. She'd also just gained an athletic
scholarship to the University of California at Berkeley
(Cal for short). Alex chose the university because
it was quirky and bohemian – different to the quiet
suburbs she lived in at Diamond Bar – but above all
else, she'd picked it for its brilliant soccer team and
high academic reputation.

Her parents had agreed it was the right choice.

'I know your heart is set on soccer as a professional career,' said her mum, Pamela, 'but you'll need something else to fall back on, just in case.'

'Mom, I know life won't always be about soccer. I want to make sure I've other options too.'

Everything was falling into place for Alex. She felt incredibly blessed and happy as the whistle blew to kick off the game. Without a care in the world, she flew down the pitch looking for opportunities to attack. As she chased down the defender on the men's side, the phrase that her dad used to say – 'Anything can happen in a minute' – was far from her mind. But she was about to find out just how true this was.

Within seconds of reaching the player and blocking his kick Alex felt a sharp pain tear through her knee. As she fell to the ground in excruciating pain and clutched her leg, a feeling of panic set in – what if this was the injury all footballers feared? Had she torn her ACL – her anterior cruciate ligament?

'I need some help! Something's not right!' Alex cried to the player next to her.

'I'm so sorry, Alex!'

'It's okay, I just – aagh! Please get some help!'

Alex's dad made sure he always came to each and every practice. As she finally managed to stand and hobbled along to the sidelines she knew he would be by her side shortly. The thought of this comforted her a little. He'd know what to do.

'You're going to be okay, honey, it's all going to be fine,' said Michael.

Alex tried not to burst into tears on him as she heard his voice and felt his arms around her. As they drove to the hospital she tried to keep the worst thoughts at bay but they kept flooding her mind:

'If I can't play soccer I'll lose my scholarship to Cal. I won't be able to finish my season with Cypress... what if I'm out of the game forever?'

She realised yet again just how much she loved soccer, but also realised what a huge part of her life it was. It had taught her so much about focusing and setting targets – and the difference that working hard and embracing the right attitude could make.

She cried out desperately: 'Please, please. Don't let this be the end for me and football!'

Her mum comforted her at the hospital while they waited for the MRI results.

'This isn't going to end your dreams, Alex. Soccer will always be a big part of your life. You're a fighter and you'll get through this. You'll beat this injury, just as you've beaten everything else.'

'She's right,' said her dad, 'this is just a setback.'

When the doctor came back in with the results, Alex took a deep breath.

'I'll give you the bad news first. It's a torn ACL that will probably require surgery. But the good news is...'

'Yes?'

'...You'll be back on the field in six months.'

Alex exhaled deeply. She could get through this, she knew people who had come back from worse and still gone on to play brilliantly.

Her parents sighed with relief too.

'We're going to take care of you. But you've got to take good care of yourself too.'

'Lots of movies, hot chocolates and ice creams!' said Alex.

She looked at her parents – her dad with his kind brown eyes and beard that he'd had as long as she could remember, and her mum with the biggest reassuring smile on her face. She loved them both so much in that moment.

But Alex knew the next six months would make her very impatient, so she made a promise to herself:

'Alex, this injury is going to make you a stronger person. All you want to do is play soccer, but you can't do that right now. Instead, you need to learn to deal with disappointment and adversity and make the best of the situation.'

CHAPTER 6

GOLDEN BEARS

'Come on guys – get to it!' Alex yelled from the sidelines to her Cypress teammates. 'Call that running? That's barely a jog!'

'Hey! Alex!' They all went rushing over to greet her. 'We've missed you!'

'Well hey, I'm gonna be here for every practice. Sure, I might not be able to do much but I'm your captain and I'm not quitting on you yet!'

Alex was devastated she'd never have the chance to play with them again but she was trying to be as cheerful as possible.

'When will you be back, Alex?' They all wanted to hear that she was recovering quickly. But frustratingly, Alex had very little to say.

'I gotta say, if I watch another episode of *Prison Break*, I'm going to explode with boredom!' She was so used to being active that sitting around watching TV felt incredibly strange to her. Still, she was doing physical therapy three times a week and slowly getting back into running, with a knee brace.

'You're responding really well,' her therapists told her. 'We're really pleased with your progress but please don't push yourself.'

'I won't,' promised Alex. She meant it. She knew her limits and was determined to take care of her body.

Within five months, she was back on the field. She didn't feel as strong or as confident on the pitch as she had done. She knew that would take longer. But the time out had reminded her just how much she loved soccer. And she had a whole new exciting chapter ahead of her at Cal. Yes, she was flying the nest and leaving her hometown, but she couldn't wait for all the adventures she knew were just around the corner.

*

Alex's dad lugged her suitcase through the airport to check in. 'Alex – exactly how many sweaters have you actually packed in here? You're not going to Siberia!'

'It's colder in Berkeley, Dad,' retorted Alex.

'You're only six hours' drive away, honey, I don't think it turns Arctic out there!'

'But Dad! That's long enough!' She turned to face her parents.

Her mum gave her a huge hug. 'It's going to be so strange without you, Alex.' She was the last of the three daughters to fly the nest so she knew this would hit them both. But at the same time, her dad was still planning to travel to all her games.

He just looked at her, smiled and said: 'Okay, Ali Cat, see you in a few weeks!'

*

Alex walked through the campus of Berkeley, beaming as she took in all the new sights – the green pristine lawns, red roofs and arches, with beautiful views across to San Francisco Bay. She was happy to be away from home and out of her comfort zone – the city itself, aside from the university, felt so diverse, new and exciting. Her mum had always said, 'Education happens outside the classroom, as much as inside it.'

But of course, Alex's biggest excitement was reserved for joining the California Golden Bears, Berkeley's soccer team. She was happy to be sharing a room with the goalkeeper Jorden LaFontaine-Kussmann who she quickly struck up a friendship with. Together, they bounded down to the first practice in their yellow-and-black strip, eager to get started. They had a new coach – Neil McGuire, who she warmed to immediately, not least for his Scottish accent. She respected the big ambitions he had for the team straight away.

'Okay, team,' Neil stated. 'I want us to win the NCAA this year!' NCCA stood for the National Collegiate Athletic Association, and they had made it to the second round the year before. Alex knew she could contribute to his dream. She already had a big goal – to be the team's best scorer.

This proved not to be straightforward, though. In the first few weeks Alex was on the sidelines again, with a sprained ankle.

She discussed her frustrations with her dad on the phone.

'How am I going to get better? I've already missed four games!'

'Honey, I think this just feels more of a blow than it really is because of the ACL injury. Get this into perspective. You can still become a professional athlete.'

'How?'

'Take this opportunity to focus on the team, rather than yourself. What are they doing? How do they pass to each other? What's their strategy? Watch them play and figure out what you can add to the team.'

She took these words in as she watched her team from the sidelines and had to smile. Her dad was right again. Out there on the field, she would be in her own head. As she took some time out, she started preparing – and plotting a strategy for the team.

CHAPTER 7

GOALS AND ACCOLADES

Neil took Alex aside in the changing room for a pep talk.

'Now Alex, I know it's your first game back after your injury and you want to prove yourself, but go easy, okay. There's no point forcing it.'

Alex nodded in agreement.

'Okay, Neil, don't worry.' It was kind of him to be concerned but she was feeling fitter and more confident than she had in a year. She felt ready to fight out on that pitch and get a chance to show them what she was made of.

The Bears were playing Saint Mary's, a college about about ten miles from Oakland. As Alex strode out on to the pitch she thought of the endless sessions where she'd practised finishing with her dad and then with Dave. 'You've worked for this, you've practised for this, you can do this,' she told herself. She could already see the angles she needed to go for as she analysed the layout of the pitch.

As the whistle blew, the only objective on her mind was winning. The hurdles of the past year – the ACL injury, the sprain – fell away from her. It felt wonderful to run around the pitch again, with the wind in her hair. No-one could reach her as she pelted up and down the field. Her confidence and her determination to seize the ball were back. She couldn't stop smiling.

In the second minute she picked up a pass from midfield. She dribbled the ball at speed down the left wing and into the penalty area. She was on her own, with defenders lagging far behind her. She saw the goalkeeper stagger to the left and right, attempting to judge where she'd take the shot. 'Don't look at their eyes!' Alex said to herself, before she booted the ball with her left foot into the goal.

GOAL!!!

Her teammates fell about her, whooping and cheering. Alex was so relieved to score her first goal of the season with the Bears. But she knew she had more to come. She went on to score two more goals in the game – a hat-trick! She was overjoyed as she celebrated with the team afterwards. It wasn't often a player got three goals in a row, but it felt incredible when it happened.

She burst into laughter when she saw Neil.

'Okay, I know I said I'd take it easy. But that was so much fun!'

'Hey, ignore my advice. That was amazing play, Alex! To score so early too! And guess what – that's the first time the team's scored a hat-trick in three years!'

'Yes!' screamed Alex, punching the air with her fists.

A few months later, in the NCCA Tournament, they faced Santa Clara University, who had been undefeated that season. The Bears conceded no goals and Alex scored the winning goal against their rivals.

After the game, she was named Soccer America's Player of the Week.

But then they played Stanford, another tough team. At half-time they were 1–0 down.

'Okay, guys,' said Neil, 'the game is far from over – we've beaten really tough competition this season. There's a great chance we can come back from this.'

But as the match went on, the Bears still couldn't find any way in on the attack. Alex glanced at the clock. There were only two minutes left in regulation time. Surely it couldn't be over? She could feel the team flagging, as though they'd already accepted defeat. She stuck her head down and said to herself: 'No, it's never over. Not till the whistle blows. Come on Alex – shake it up. You've still got some energy left – use it.'

She was down near the penalty box when she picked up a pass from midfield. It was a split-second choice: pass to her teammate who was closer, or take the shot herself. She chose to shoot.

GOAL!!! Alex had equalised with just over a minute to go. Her teammates were ecstatic to level the game, but now they faced extra time. With neither side scoring, it went into penalty kicks where the Bears lost out.

Neil consoled them after the match. 'I'm really proud of how you all played. You really kept your end up against a tough side. I think with a bit more work, we'll take the title next season.'

'Especially if Alex keeps scoring like that,' said one of the girls.

Alex blushed.

'Yeah – so late in the game! Amazing!' said another.

'She's a real game changer,' said Neil. 'We need players who can surprise like that and turn things around in the final minutes.'

Alex called her dad that evening with the news.

'Oh honey, I'm sorry.'

'It's okay, Dad, I think we played really well. And Dad, guess what?'

'What?'

'I've scored more goals than any other Cal player this year.'

'That's terrific, honey!'

Alex was very happy. One of the first goals she'd set herself was to be the top scorer that year and she'd achieved it already, early in her freshman year. But she knew it wasn't just down to her own hard work. She put together a list of all the people she was grateful to – her coach, her teammates and her dad. She smiled as she wrote it out – it was growing longer all the time.

CHAPTER 8

CHILE

Alex was shaking with nerves as she stood on the pitch at Home Depot Center. She'd been called up to the US women's national Under-20 soccer team for training. This was what she'd been waiting for, another step on her journey to becoming a professional player. But the excitement she'd initially felt had soon faded, quickly replaced by the weight of expectation and fear.

'Get it together Alex, come on!' She tried to steady herself as practice kicked off. But for the first time in a long while she felt out of her depth and overwhelmed. She hadn't played on a national team since her ACL injury, and didn't feel she was up to the same standard as the other players.

She left the training angry and disappointed with herself. It was a relief to get back to her Cal teammates.

'Maybe I'm just not cut out for this, Dad! Who was I trying to kid?' she said, trying to hold back the tears on the phone to him.

'Alex, stop being so hard on yourself. You are good enough for the national team. You are. I think your nerves just got the better of you. And you may be surprised. I'm sure they saw something unique in you, despite your nerves.'

'No, Dad. I messed up. I just know it. I've missed my chance to play for the U-20 World Cup. And it's all my fault.'

*

'Is this Alex Morgan?'

Alex recognised the voice at the end of the phone. Could it be one of the coaches from the training camp? Her stomach lurched.

'Yes?'

'We've a spot available for the World Cup

qualifying tournament. Someone had to drop off the team.'

Alex nearly dropped her phone.

'What? Wow! I thought I played so badly.'

'Well, yes, you were the last player we added,' the coach said crisply.

'Oh, thank you! Thank you for believing in...'

The coach had already hung up. But she didn't mind.

'Thank you for this second chance,' she said out loud. 'I'm going to play the best soccer of my life. I swear it.'

*

Alex had worked incredibly hard over the previous few months in the qualifying tournament and friendly games, to prove she was ready for the opportunity to represent her country in the 2008 Under-20s World Cup in Chile. She held her breath as the team's coach Tony DiCicco began to read the names out for the roster, and jumped for joy as her name was read out. She'd been picked to play as a forward, on the starter roster.

'Alex – we're so, so proud of you!' her parents
cried down the phone.

'Thank you, Mom, thank you, Dad!'

'We can't wait to come and see you in Chile!'

*

'Wow! Just wow!'

In Chile, Alex and her teammates gazed in
disbelief at the packed stadium that surrounded them
before their match against Argentina.

'This is incredible! The South Americans really do
love their soccer, don't they?' said Sydney Leroux.
The team were used to playing much smaller crowds.
But the host country Chile had put a huge amount of
effort and energy into the U-20 Women's World Cup,
rebuilding four new stadiums.

Alex shook her head and laughed. 'I wish this
was being televised. People back home wouldn't
believe it.'

She was always happy to know that her parents –
if not both of them, at least her dad – were always in
the crowd. It helped her to play better, knowing he
was always there. But she felt so proud tonight that,

for once, they were watching her play in a huge crowd.

'Let's give all of them something to remember!' shouted Sydney.

Despite Argentina's long history and love for the game, the USA team didn't find them difficult to beat. Alex scored a long shot in the first half and then again in the ninetieth minute, easily crushing the opposition in a 3–0 defeat.

'I heard you were a late-game scorer!' Tony congratulated her in the after-match celebrations.

The team continued to sail through the tournament, beating England and Germany. Alex had to pinch herself as she sang the US national anthem in her first major international final. They were set to play North Korea, a great team who'd won back in 2006.

The USA team felt the pressure from the North Koreans immediately. Even when Sydney scored a long shot in the first half hour they sensed they were in it for the long haul. Alex knew this wouldn't be easy: 'Stay focused team, stay focused.'

But just before half-time she saw a chance open up for her. She picked up a throw-in from her teammate Ellie on the right side and heard the fans erupt with cheers as she got control of it. Caught between two defenders, she dribbled past them and nearly lost the ball to another. Another tried to chase her down but she cut inside and passed her.

Alex looked up. 'The goal is at least twenty-six yards away! Can I make it? Oh – just go for it!'

She wobbled slightly as she lifted her left foot to aim. 'Oh no – have I blown it?' She watched with wonder and disbelief as she got her answer. The ball sailed perfectly towards the far post and went in.

GOAL!!!

She started to laugh as relief, joy and disbelief hit her all at once. She felt tears well up in her as the team leapt around her.

'That was amazing, Alex!'

'I can't believe it went in!' gushed Alex. She could barely get the words out.

They held on throughout the match. The North Koreans scored in the ninety-second minute, but it was too late. Almost straight away the referee blew the whistle.

Alex lay awake that night, almost in a state of shock and disbelief. She'd had the most incredible evening celebrating with her team and family. At the age of nineteen, she'd achieved a goal that she'd dreamt about for so long. She was part of the US team that had won the Under-20 Women's World Cup. And she'd done it through sheer hard work and determination.

'Please though, I've one more dream,' she said as she gazed out of the window staring at the stars, basking in what a glorious day it had been. 'Let me join the women's national team. I want us to win the World Cup too.'

CHAPTER 9

A KNEE-JERK REACTION

'Wow! Look! There's the lake!' The whole of the
Cal Golden Bears team craned their heads in awe as
the tour bus steered towards the sparkling blue of
Lake Como in Italy, around winding mountains, past
terracotta-tiled roofs and quaint churches.

'Everything is just so old!'

'The buildings are so beautiful!'

'There's nothing like this in the States.'

'I wish!'

For many of the team, including Alex, it was
their first trip to Europe playing exhibition games
across Italy, Switzerland and Ireland. She was having
the time of her life on these travels, experiencing

different cultures and lifestyles. She loved to be thrown out of her comfort zone, not least because it helped to develop her style of play.

Neil had warned her to watch out for the Italians' strong defensive tactics, especially as she was an attacker.

'I'll be fine!' she'd laughed. But one match with them proved his point when she struggled to get through their rigid defence.

'Yeah, okay, I see what you mean! They're very tactical.'

'It's called *catenaccio* – meaning "doorbolt". Nothing can get through!'

Alex loved learning and picking up skills from other international players.

'It's amazing,' she reflected. 'This game is played all over the world – yet every country has its own unique and different way of doing it.'

'Just wait till you play the Brazilians one day!' said Neil. 'One of the best sides in the world!'

'Oh I can't wait!' Alex replied. 'And we'll thrash them!' Her dream of playing on the national team in

the World Cup was still very much alive in her heart.
But for now, she was enjoying the summer and was
even prepared to take some time off from playing
football. Before returning to university, she travelled
to Madrid to study Spanish, as part of her degree
in political economy. She had another goal – to be
fluent by the time she returned.

'How was Barcelona, honey?'

'Barça, Dad – Barça! That's what they call the
team out there!'

'Well of course, I'm sorry, now that you're fluent
and all!'

'Dad – they were incredible! And that Messi? He
really is as brilliant in the flesh! Easily my favourite
player now – he's just on a different level.'

'It sounds as though you're having a great time.'

'Dad, it's been a blast. I've had so much fun out
here – I've eaten tapas, danced flamenco, and yes,
spoken some Spanish!'

'Are you fluent now?'

'Of course, Dad... I mean, *por supuesto!*'

'You're not going to want to come back!'

'Oh Dad, no, I'm ready to return. And I want to give the Bears my all this year.'

It was true. She was missing playing with the team at Cal and couldn't wait for pre-season training to start. Her World Cup dreams could wait a while.

*

The mood in the locker room at half-time was not great. The Bears were 1–0 down against Sacramento State, a team they were expected to beat. This followed one week after a loss to Cal Poly, which had seen them drop in the rankings. They'd been working so hard on their technical abilities with the assistant coaches but they were halfway through the season and not making headway.

As they sat waiting for half-time instructions, Alex could feel how deflated the team were. Then the unexpected happened. Their coach Neil sloped in through the back door. He avoided looking them in the eye before stating: 'This isn't working for me. I'm out.' He then left.

The girls stared after him in utter disbelief before turning to each other.

'Is he for real?'

'How can he do this?' Alex felt tears of rage well up in her eyes as she stared around at the dejected team. How could he leave them, when they were at their lowest ebb? She'd just started to feel as though she really trusted Neil, especially since the summer they'd all spent together as a team. And now he was going in the middle of a game? But as team leader, Alex knew she had to hold it together for the girls, especially for the younger players.

'Okay, girls, this is a huge shock, I know. But we've got to put this aside for the next forty-five minutes, get out there and show them.'

But there were too many negative feelings of anger and hurt milling around in their heads. It was impossible to concentrate on the game and play their best soccer. After the game, Alex went back to her room feeling even more hurt and angry. She needed to vent. And at that moment Twitter felt like the best way to do it. She went to her page and wrote: 'you turned your back on us once. We can and will turn our backs on you for good.'

As she clicked to post, she felt some of the anger subside. And even more subsided as retweets and messages of support flooded in. But the relief was short-term. She had a restless night's sleep and woke up to a message from her dad asking her to call. Her heart sank a little.

'Alex,' he started, 'what's going on? It isn't like you to lose your cool.'

Alex began to garble a defensive response in between angry tears, then realised he had a point. It wasn't like her, not really. She'd let her emotions take control of her and cloud her judgement.

'I'm sorry, Dad, I just... I just felt so angry.'

'Hey, I know, I understand. But next time, take some time out. Call us, talk to us, you don't have to go through these things alone.'

'You're right. It was a knee-jerk reaction.'

'I know you're hurt but you'll get through this. These things have a way of working out okay.'

Alex regretted the Twitter post, but knew there was little point wallowing in what was done. She headed off to Saturday morning practice determined to stay positive. Kelly Lindsay, their assistant coach, was stepping in as head coach. She was there to greet them with a pep talk.

'I know that yesterday was terrible,' she began. 'But team work is going to save the day. Players make a team.'

Two days later, the Bears played Santa Clara. They were disappointed when the match ended in a draw, but they played the best that they could – and as a team. Alex knew they'd soon be back winning games again.

CHAPTER 10

LIFE IS FULL OF SURPRISES

'I'm so sorry I put you all in this position. What I did was wrong and I owe each and every one of you an apology.'

Alex stared in shock and disbelief at Neil as he addressed the team. She knew there was little time to dwell as the regular season began that week. There was no choice but to let go of grudges for the sake of the team. They couldn't change the past and he was here to stay. But she still felt incredibly angry. At the end of training, Neil took her to one side.

'Can we talk, Alex?'

She stared him right in the eyes. She thought of her family and how they'd always been right behind her. 'No-one's ever given up on me like that before.'

'I know,' he replied. 'And I'm really sorry. I know it's going to take time to win your trust back.'

'Yes, but I realise this isn't just about me. We've got games to play and we want to win them.'

'Okay.'

They both managed to crack a smile. The next morning Alex posted on Twitter, ahead of the PAC-10 tournament: 'Leaving for Oregon. Ready for the bears to go get 'em!' It always felt better to think as positively as possible.

'Okay, guys – let's do this!' she shouted as they ran out on to the field. She felt a shift in their energy on the field and the way they were listening and responding to each other. Just before half-time she set up an assist for the midfielder. Oregon levelled in the second half but Alex, true to form, nailed home a goal ten minutes before time. They didn't relax or let their game fall until the whistle blew. Then they let the sheer relief and joy of winning pour over them. Alex was thrilled.

'Girls, it's been a rollercoaster of a past week but

no-one would ever know, given how we just played out there today!'

With no injuries or national team commitments, Alex played every single game in the season. The Bears were ousted by number one-seeded Florida State in the second round of the NCCA Tournament, but Alex was nevertheless proud of how the team had played throughout. And praise for her style of play continued to flood in from the coaches. As they all noted, her time with the national team had enhanced her overall ability, making her a much more mature and complete player. In particular, she'd developed a knack for finishing with both feet and with sixteen goals to her name that season, she was continuously described as 'Cal's biggest scoring threat'.

Her bond with Neil had also strengthened. He'd been an incredible support to her throughout the season and she felt as though her trust in him was returning.

'You know, Dad, it's funny,' said Alex on the phone for their weekly check-in, and said of Neil, 'I think we're better friends than we were before.'

'Life is full of surprises, honey.'

*

It was the morning of Thanksgiving, the most important American national holiday, and Alex was back home relaxing in Diamond Bar with her family.

'It's such a treat to have you all back under one roof,' said her mum, as Alex came downstairs in her pyjamas to help her start on the cooking.

'Talking of treats, can I make funfetti cake too?' asked Alex.

'Well, sure, you bake the best there is! Because I taught you, of course.'

Alex adored this time of year. It was a rare time to switch off, eat great food and catch up with old friends.

She was busy chopping some vegetables when her phone rang. She didn't recognise the number but picked it up anyway.

'Alex, this is Cheryl Bailey.' Alex's heart skipped a beat. Cheryl was the general manager of the women's national team.

'We'd like you to come train with us,' Cheryl

continued. 'I hope you're ready – you will be working every day!'

Alex took a deep breath before answering. 'Yes! Thank you! I'll be there! I'm honoured.'

When she hung up the phone, she jumped around the kitchen for joy, hugging her parents and practically lifting them both off the floor. Cheryl had asked if she was healthy, but she felt strong enough to move an entire mountain at that moment.

'This is the best Thanksgiving ever! The best day ever! I'm so excited!' Alex knew in her heart she'd soon be playing competition and friendly games with the national team, which could take her to the World Cup or the Olympics. She suspected she'd get this call one day, but it had come earlier than she'd anticipated.

Her parents had tears in their eyes.

'You've worked so hard for this, Alex – all these years!' cried her dad.

Alex looked at them both and thought back on all the days practising shooting goals with her dad, late into the evening, even though he had to leave the house every morning at 5:30am to work at his construction company. She thought of all the practices her mum had driven her to. And they'd only ever supported her dream. They'd never complained. It seemed so fitting to be with them here at this moment, on Thanksgiving.

'I'm so lucky to have you as my parents,' she said, before hugging them again, tears of happiness pouring down her face.

CHAPTER 11

RECOGNITION FOR BABY HORSE

'Alex – welcome!'

Alex looked into the warm, open face of Pia Sundhage, the US head coach, as she came striding towards her. With bright blue eyes and a huge smile on her face, Pia was a legend in her native Sweden – and one of the national team's best forwards, so her reputation preceded her.

As friendly as Pia and the team were, Alex suddenly felt intimidated as she looked around at the players – she was standing in the company of giants. There was the towering forward Abby Wambach – nine years Alex's senior, she was one of the best players in the game. Then there was Hope Solo, regarded as one of the best female goalkeepers in the world.

Alex felt some of her old shyness from childhood returning and doubts began to flood her mind. 'What if they just think I'm a baby?' She was the youngest there after all. Her thoughts returned to the U-20 training camp when her nerves had got the better of her. She couldn't let them get the better of her again.

When Pia spoke to her, it was as if she could read her mind. 'It's so good to finally meet you. I saw you play in Chile at the final.'

'Wow,' thought Alex, briefly reassured, 'she was in the crowd watching.'

To some degree, she was going to be too busy for nerves. The training camp was ten days long and she was in the middle of her university exams. She would have to study straight after a practice, plus two friendly games every day.

'Are you serious, Alex, can you do this?' she asked herself. 'Yes I can,' she answered. 'Alex, you've always juggled the different priorities in your life.'

By the end of the first day she was completely

exhausted as she strived to keep up with her teammates' higher level of playing. But everyone was encouraging and embraced the unique skills they saw that she could bring to the team.

'So this is why we needed a younger player, eh?' said Abby. 'With speed like that you're in danger of making us feel like a pack of old tortoises!'

'We need her to teach us how to run!'

'Incredible speed!' exclaimed Hope. 'Like a baby horse!'

Alex laughed. She was soon to find out that 'Baby Horse' was going to stick to her as an affectionate nickname, whether she liked it or not. But she wasn't the only fast one on the team; each morning she would swap striker tactics and tips with the other forward, Amy Rodriguez. And she immediately struck up a friendship with her roommate – midfielder Heather O'Reilly, who always seemed to be smiling and had boundless energy.

Heather was reassuring too. 'I was so nervous on my first day of training camp I could barely kick a ball,' she said. 'We all think you're doing really well.'

Each day got easier for Alex. Her entire field of vision was opening up as she became more tactical and technical. And as well as the playing, she also enjoyed the moments where they all sat down to eat together as a team and reflect on the games they'd played.

At the end of the ten days Pia took her aside. 'You're doing great, Alex – we're really impressed. I could tell you were nervous but you didn't let it get to you. On top of studying for your finals you've really thrown yourself into the challenge here.'

'I'm learning so much from the team,' replied Alex. 'I've never played with anyone this good before.'

'Well, they think you're pretty exceptional too. How'd you like a spot on the national team?'

Alex was almost too excited to sit her exams after this offer but managed to focus her concentration for the few more weeks that she needed to. That Christmas at home she didn't really feel as though she wanted or needed any gifts. She'd already received the best one of all.

*

'I'm the only college player they've asked, Dad!'

'Alex, that's amazing, well done.'

'It's a huge honour, HUGE.' Alex was feeling excited but overwhelmed. It was the new year and she was one of twenty-six players that had been called up to train at another national team training camp at the Home Depot Center. From there, Pia would pick nineteen players for the Algarve Cup, an important championship in women's football, held in Portugal every year.

'This could be my first senior international tournament!' Alex told her dad. 'I really want to be picked!'

'How will you fit this in with your studies, honey?'

Alex wasn't sure. As excited as she was, she also felt overwhelmed at the prospect of juggling both. She'd have to miss three weeks of classes and study back at the hotel.

'I'm just going to have to balance my time better than I've ever done before, Dad. And try to focus on one thing at a time. When I'm on the field, I must concentrate 100 per cent on soccer – off the pitch it's school.'

'You've always managed it before, Alex. But remember, if you don't get picked for the Cup, you've still got your senior year of Cal ahead of you.'

'Dad, I know – whatever happens I'm lucky to be playing soccer every day, whether it's with the Bears or the national team.'

*

It was the third day of training at the camp. Alex was incredibly happy to see all the new friends again that she'd made on the team and was enjoying the day of practice. But as she was running down the field she felt a sharp pain in the back of her leg. She skidded to a halt and bent down trying to stretch it out. The pain grew worse.

'Oh no, I hope it's not my hamstring,' she said. It was a common area for runners to strain. She hobbled off to the sides to have her leg examined, where the trainers confirmed she'd hurt it.

'Do you think I can continue playing?' asked Alex. She really didn't want to miss practice or go home.

'We'll wrap your leg tight in a compression, then see how you feel.'

Alex started to sprint again but immediately felt pain. She'd strained it even more and it was going to be a couple of weeks before she was back on the field.

She felt broken-hearted. At twenty, she was the youngest player at the camp but also the youngest to leave.

Amy and Heather hugged her goodbye and comforted her: 'Don't worry Alex, you'll recover soon. Hamstring injuries don't take too long to heal.' She tried not to well up at their kind words.

Alex spent the next few weeks healing and focusing on her studies. Every day she checked in on the Algarve Cup results and cheered on her teammates in spirit to their hard-fought final against Germany.

Her hamstring recovered quicker than she was expecting. She missed playing, of course, but as with her last injury, the time off helped her to appreciate her love and passion for the sport even more.

However, she hoped she didn't have too long to wait until she had another chance to play with the team.

'They won't forget about me, will they, Dad?'

'Be patient, Alex.'

It wasn't long till she heard Cheryl's voice on the end of the phone again. 'We'd like you to play a friendly against Mexico.'

Alex grinned from ear to ear. She couldn't wait to get back out there.

CHAPTER 12

WORKING TOWARDS A GOAL

'Well, this is going to be a new challenge!' Alex thought to herself as the team landed in Utah. She looked out of the window and shivered. The snow was falling thick and fast.

Abby looked at her and smiled. 'Ah, Californian girl, you'll get used to it.'

'I've never played in snow before!' said Alex.

'Well, think of the poor Mexican players, they've probably not even seen it before!' said Pia.

'Oh, I can't wait!' said Alex. And she couldn't. It was her first international game and she'd been told she'd play forty-five minutes at least. It was likely she'd be playing for the entire second half.

'My dream is really coming true!' Alex thought.

But even better than that, she was about to meet one of her long-time heroes – Kristine Lilly. As a ten-year-old, all those years before, Alex had watched Kristine play in the World Cup on the TV screen. Kristine had taken a few years off from the national team but decided she wanted to come back. Now here she was – one of the women's team's best scorers, wearing her Number 13 shirt.

Alex couldn't believe she was about to play alongside her. She was even more shocked when Kristine greeted her so warmly:

'Hello Alex – great to have you on the team!'

Alex struggled a little to look her in the eye. She was awestruck. But Kristine was so bright and breezy that she managed to shake her hand. And before she knew it the words were tumbling out of her mouth. 'Kristine, this means so much to me. As a little girl I watched you play in that final and just wanted to be you. I've always worn Number 13 in your honour.'

'Well Alex,' she replied with a huge smile, 'when I retire, Number 13 is yours.'

Kristine's words were still ringing in her ears as they all stood watching the snow fall, waiting for the game to begin. Three inches had already settled and conditions would be awful to play in, but so what? Alex couldn't believe how lucky she was as she stared around at her team. She hadn't played with them for very long, but she already felt she had a strong bond with the players.

Just before they braced for the snow, Abby turned to them and said: 'Okay, guys, if we score, we're doing snow angels. And if we go two up, it's snowball-fight time.'

They all laughed. They'd make the best they could of playing in the snow because they were a team.

For the first half, Alex watched them play from the sidelines.

'Oh, look at the ball!' cried one of the team. 'It's yellow!' Conditions were so bad they had to use a bright colour so that the players could see it.

In the forty-sixth minute Alex took to the field. They were yet to score, but she couldn't be happier as she and the team slid all over the place, snow in their eyes and sloshing up their legs. She tried to make several passes but the ball would roll and get stuck.

As neither side scored, they began to wonder if it was just impossible to score. Finally, in the sixtieth minute, Abby managed to tap in a goal a yard from the goal. True to her word, she ran to the right corner of the field where she lay down and started making snow angels. Alex was overcome with joy as she ran with the rest of the team to lie down beside her and join in. Who would have thought that hard work could be this much fun? They won against Mexico 1–0, and Alex knew it was a day she would never forget.

*

The 2011 Women's World Cup was just a year away, and if Alex was to make her dream of playing soccer professionally come true, she had some difficult decisions to make. She knew it was likely she'd be picked for a team for the Women's Professional Soccer league (WPS). She also knew she had to concentrate fully on this. As usual, she talked it over with her parents.

'Is soccer what you really love?'

'Well of course, Dad.'

'I think working on both college and soccer is going to become too much for you. You're not a superhero, Alex – as much as I wonder sometimes!'

'You know what, Dad? I think I've made my decision. I'm going to graduate early.'

Alex knew that a lot of collegiate athletes had left college to pursue sports full-time, but her education was still important to her. If she took classes during the summer she could finish in the autumn term. Then she'd have plenty of time to prepare for the World Cup.

'You know what, Alex,' her dad sighed. 'It's a good thing you like multi-tasking.'

'I can do this,' she replied.

It was a tough summer. Alex juggled extra classes, played friendly games with the national team and practised soccer every day. But she enjoyed it because she was working towards a goal – to graduate early and move on to playing professionally, doing what she loved the most. The multi-tasking was rewarded too, as she made the Hermann Trophy shortlist again (awarded to top collegiate soccer players) and was chosen as a Lowe's Senior Class Awards candidate – a prize awarded to students who'd excelled in community, classroom, character and competition.

But despite her decision, she still felt a mix of emotions as she stood on the field before the first game of the season. She had bittersweet feelings about leaving the Cal Bears.

'Live Like Champions' – it was the motto Neil had instilled in the team and it had really helped to consolidate all that Alex had achieved that year. It wasn't just about getting the best GPA (grade point average) of any team but about putting your best foot forward, on the field and off.

'We can't believe you're going this early,' said Neil.

Alex hung her head. 'This team has taught me so much.' Indeed – it had taken her to Europe and brought her soccer game to a whole new level, helping her get to where she wanted to be.

'Thank you, Neil. I may be gone for some time, but I want to give back to this team.'

'You'd better!' he replied, although he didn't doubt it. Even when Alex had a guaranteed spot on the national team, she'd continued doing individual drills with the Bears after every practice.

Her graduation was only a few months away, but she was determined to play her heart out for the last season. She scored a hat-trick in one game and scored five goals in one weekend. By mid-September 2010 they were unbeaten with a record of five wins and three ties. Alex was leaving on a high.

CHAPTER 13

GREAT TEAMWORK

'Okay, we've got two friendly games with China coming up – can you come to Atlanta for training with us?'

Barely a month into her senior year, Alex was off again. Alex knew these matches were important for a number of reasons. Yes, they were warm-ups before the World Cup qualifying tournament and a chance to bond with the team and work on tactics. But Alex knew this was no time to get complacent either – her place on the World Cup qualifying roster wasn't guaranteed. These were similar to tryouts, so she had to prove herself.

However, this time around she felt a lot more at

home with the team. It was her third training camp and she felt as though she was meeting up with old friends. Plus she wasn't the only collegiate player there this time. Sydney Leroux, who she'd played with in the U-20 World Cup, was also there. It had already been two years and she couldn't wait to catch up with her.

She was particularly looking forward to playing with Abby again too. The entire team appreciated her positivity off and on the pitch – as their top scorer she combined great power with technical skill and was renowned for her ability to shoot brilliant headers. Alex had always felt a strong connection with her on the pitch, but it was during these practices that she realised it was strengthening.

Pia was noticing it too. 'I think we've got a winning combination here,' she remarked to Alex. 'The opposition won't know what's hit them – with your speed and Abby's energy.'

Neither player could wait to put this into practice for real.

*

Alex's face fell a little. She hadn't been picked as a starter for the game against China. They were playing in Chester, Pennsylvania, outside of Philadelphia, at PPL Park.

Pia reassured her. 'Alex, you're a brilliant mid-to-late game threat. I know if I put you on the field in the second half you'll really shake things up. Plus, you're fast. When everyone's flagging at the end of the game, those legs pick up everyone's energy out there.'

Alex was pleased to hear this and knew that Pia was thinking strategically, but a part of her wanted to prove that she could play consistently well from start to finish.

She couldn't help but feel a little frustrated sitting on the sidelines, but she did her best to distract herself by warming up and cheering on the team. Her parents were in the crowd too and she knew they'd be rooting for her as soon as she got on the pitch.

The US side started off strong but the game took a turn for the worse when China scored in the thirty-seventh minute with a twelve-yard volley. When they reached half-time Alex was itching to get out and play, to make a difference.

Pia looked at her. 'Stay calm, Alex, I'm going to put you and Yael on soon.'

In the seventy-first minute, Alex finally got her chance to play when she and defender Yael Averbuch were put on. As they ran out they turned to each other and said: 'Okay – let's lift this game!'

With the pair's arrival on the field, Alex immediately felt the energy change. The team played differently – they were starting to attack in a way they hadn't in the first half.

It was the eighty-third minute. Yael picked up the ball and tapped it to Heather. She lobbed it hard over the line of Chinese defence, where it landed in front of Abby who sprinted down the field towards the goal. She then headed it in Alex's direction.

Alex sped towards it and dribbled it for a few more yards with her left foot. As space opened up for her she told herself: 'Aim with your left foot Alex – you know it's your best, your most precise. And it always throws people off.' Then: 'Don't look the goalkeeper in the eyes or give away where you're shooting.' These were the mantras that ran through her mind every time she shot.

'Take it – do it now!' She smacked the ball with her left foot and watched as it finished up in the left corner, exactly where she wanted it to go.

GOAL!!!!

She'd done it. She'd scored her first international goal with the senior team. She was only twenty-one, the only college player on the team, and she'd rescued their game. Everything that she'd ever worked towards had built up to this moment. She thought of her family leaping up and down in the stands and she felt joy and happiness fall in waves all around her. It was the happiest she'd ever felt in her life.

As she turned around to look for her teammates she saw Kristine Lilly with her arms outstretched running towards her: 'Go Alex – you go girl!'

Alex fell into the arms of her childhood idol, and a feeling of total euphoria swept over her. How fitting and meaningful this moment felt for her. It was an honour to be on the field with her, but to be congratulated by her meant everything.

'Great teamwork, guys,' said Pia, after the match. 'You know, we were close to losing on US soil there for a minute, something we've not done in six years. You saved the day.'

'All down to Alex's left foot,' said Abby.

'And your header!' Alex replied.

They looked at each other with a new-found respect and fondness. That match had cemented a new understanding and bond between them. Alex hoped with all her heart she'd be given the chance to prove herself again.

CHAPTER 14

MEXICO

Who would make the cut for the World Cup
qualifying team? Alex, standing with the rest of the
team, was shaking. She was about to find out if her
dream since the age of ten was about to come true.

Pia stood in front and faced them all.

'You've all worked so hard and I'm so proud of
you all. I can only choose twenty players, but please
know that you've all been amazing.'

Alex tried to steady her emotions as she heard her
name ring out through the air. 'Alex Morgan' ... it
suddenly sounded so different. She was so excited,
but she had to contain herself. Some people were

going home, so instantly celebrating didn't seem appropriate in that moment.

When Alex got back to her room she called her parents. Her voice was shaking.

'Mom, Dad, I'm on the World Cup qualifying team. We're going to Mexico to play at the end of the month.'

All the hours of practice, all the money they'd poured into teams and coaches and driving her to each game had been worth it.

Her mum began to cry. 'Alex, I am so proud of you. This is what you've been working for and you did it. You did it!'

'Remember, Mom,' said Alex through tears, 'we still have to qualify for the World Cup and I have to be chosen for the final team.'

'Whatever!' said her dad. 'You've been chosen to play for your country. We couldn't be prouder!'

Pia had drawn together a great team and Alex couldn't wait to begin playing with them when they reached Mexico. It was a great mix of older, more experienced players and newer, fresher ones.

Kristine Lilly had been to four World Cups and Abby Wambach had been to two. For more than half the team, though, it was a completely new experience.

As Pia put it: 'The veterans bring experience; the new players add inspiration.'

Alex took one last look over the red roofs of Berkeley, and the San Francisco Bay in the distance sparkling away. As she did so, a reporter from the Cal newspaper was asking her a question for an interview: 'Alex, what's the most important thing you've learned at Cal?'

'You should always work hard, never give up, and fight until the end because it's never really over until the whistle blows.'

Alex knew this was true for every single game. And she intended to keep it at the forefront of her mind on the next part of her journey.

*

With the US team about to face Mexico, Pia's pep talk was one of encouragement and concern.

'Okay, girls, you're doing great,' she told them, 'but let's not get complacent, Mexico are a good side.' The US team had reached the semi-finals of the qualifiers and deep down they felt very confident; they had never lost against Mexico.

It was hard walking out onto the pitch though. The team looked at each other and grimaced as they heard a surge of support for their opponents. They craned their necks for a few star spangled banners amongst the crowd of 8,500 fans.

'Can't see many US flags, guys!'

'Hey, we're one of the best teams in the world!'

'*The* best!'

Above it all, though, Alex was always sure she could hear her parents screaming: 'Go, Alex! Go, USA!' As long as they were behind her, she thought. She'd not been slated for the beginning of the game, but was down as a substitute for the second half.

But as she watched from the sidelines, she knew the team could play better than they were. Something wasn't quite gelling. And within two minutes, one of Mexico's best players had got past some pretty shoddy US defence. Alex looked on in horror as the player speedily nipped a shot past the goalkeeper. The US team had been caught off guard and they were already down 1–0.

Alex turned round in dismay to the other subs: 'We haven't even warmed up!'

'How did they do that?!'

'Come on, guys!' Alex cheered them on. 'You can come back from this!'

In the twenty-fifth minute, Megan Rapinoe took a corner kick. The ball soared through the air, and landed right in the middle of a crowd of players waiting in the penalty area. Alex took a deep breath as she saw Carli Lloyd slide to the ground to reach the ball as it landed in front of her, kicking it into the right side of the goal.

Phew! They had tied, 1–1. But Alex knew it was far from over. If neither side scored again, the game would slide into overtime and penalty kicks – a scenario they always dreaded. Just two minutes later, Mexican player Verónica Pérez headed the ball past Hope Solo. It was a wonderful shot – precise, fast and completely deserved.

Alex hung her head in dismay as the Mexican fans

went ballistic. It went from bad to worse as Abby collided with another player and started bleeding from the head.

The atmosphere at half-time was not good.

'How can we be 2–1 down?'

'We've always beaten them!'

'We've never missed getting into the finals of the World Cup qualifying tournament!'

Alex was determined to make a difference into the second half when she went on, but she could feel the momentum of the game had plummeted. Some shots opened up for them which they should have got in but their finishing just wasn't good enough. She tried to hold on to her 'not over till the whistle blows' motto but she felt they couldn't pull it back now. Plus, the Mexican defence was just too strong.

It was hard to face the truth that they hadn't played well enough but Alex knew the Mexican side deserved their 2–1 win.

'You guys had a tough time out there,' said Pia, 'but we can't wallow here or take too much time making excuses. We've got to learn from these mistakes and move forward.'

When the press asked Abby for a comment, she said: 'Any team, even the number one team in the world, will lose.'

She added: 'It's a wake-up call for everyone, and we're going to make sure it never happens again.'

CHAPTER 15

QUALIFYING HOPEFULS

When the USA played Italy, the atmosphere in the crowd was completely different. There were only 5,000 in the crowd, but a small group of them were American, chanting, 'USA! USA!'

Alex smiled as she saw them waving flags and cheering the team on. She warmed up on the sidelines as she watched the first half. She watched the ball go back and forth with a number of attempts at shots on goal from both sides. But by the end of the first half there was still no score.

As the second half got going, Alex paced up and down, trying to stay as calm and patient as possible. 'I just want to get out and score!' she said to the team's fitness coach.

'Keep warming up,' the coach replied, 'try to be patient.' But by the eighty-fifth minute, Alex felt as though she would burst. There was still no score, on either side. She just wanted to make a difference.

All of a sudden, Pia walked up to her, looked her in the eye and said: 'You're going in now. Just go to the goal. You don't have to be tricky. You don't have to be smart. Just go to the goal, because you're faster than everybody else.'

It reminded her of what her old club coach had always said about her before she perfected her technique: 'No skill, but all speed.'

'Well, I'm even faster now,' thought Alex, as she leapt up with delight and ran out on to the pitch.

She beamed as she heard one of her flapping teammates say, 'Hey, here comes Baby Horse!'

They were nine minutes into stoppage time. Alex kept seeking out opportunities or assists. Then she saw Abby control a long pass that she nudged off her head towards Alex.

The ball landed right in front of her. She heard Pia's instruction again: 'Just go to the goal.' She ran with the ball, as fast as possible. As she got closer to the goal, she heard the US fans cheer her on.

'Do it now Alex – now!'

She shot. And she scored.

GOAL!!! The team were 1–0 up! Alex knew this was one of the biggest and most important goals of her life. She'd taken her team to the next stage.

She ran towards her teammates and they all hugged each other on the field. They waited for the final seconds to tick by. At last the whistle blew and they all rejoiced.

'Just one more game! One more game and we're off to the World Cup!'

As they flew back to America, they reflected on their experiences in the qualifiers. They'd had both highs and lows, but they knew their second and last game against Italy would be easier. It was in Chicago so the crowd would be larger and, hopefully, friendlier.

★

Before their game in Chicago against Italy, the US team gathered together nervously for their latest pep talk with Pia.

'We have to be positive,' she said. 'None of us wanted to play these two games, and it's been tough. But we've already won one game, so we just need to go out, enjoy ourselves and play our best. This will take us all the way to Germany...'

In the changing room, Alex absorbed these words as she put her right sock on before her left one – it was a little superstition she'd gotten into the habit of before each game, along with taking a power nap at the same time in the day. She thought of what her dad often reminded her of too: 'Just imagine if everything came easily – you need the ups and downs.'

And just before the team ran out onto the pitch, she always took a few quiet minutes to visualise herself on the field too – anticipating the opportunities to shoot and score in her mind's eye. She adjusted her pink hairband – it was still one of her favourite colours – which she wore at every match and told herself: 'You may shoot five times and only get one goal. But go for it each time.'

It was a typical Chicago winter and the girls were all freezing. Alex shivered as she took her place as a sub at the sidelines. She visualised warm Californian days back at Berkeley and playing club soccer with Cypress Elite. She watched with bated breath as the whistle blew for kick-off, and the US team hit the ground running.

In the first half, her heart skipped a beat on several occasions when the ball slipped past the midfield and their defenders were placed under pressure. She sighed with relief every time when each shot on goal failed. Just before half-time she whooped for joy as Amy scored. They were 1–0 up – yes!

'The Italians really need to step it up if they want to get through now,' said Pia. Alex was relieved, though she knew it was unlikely she'd be brought on in the next half as Amy was playing so well. This was not a time to rock the boat.

Abby looked at her and smiled, sensing some of her disappointment: 'Miss you out there, Alex!'

Alex missed her, too. Abby was a tour de force out on the field and Alex was desperate to get in on the action. But as the whistle blew for the end of the match to mark the USA win at 1–0, she felt overwhelmed with relief and joy. They were through.

CHAPTER 16

ROLE MODELS

The USA team had qualified for the World Cup, but would Alex still be a part of it? By Christmas 2010, she had reached so many of her goals – graduating from college early, and playing for the national team. Even so, her inclusion in the World Cup team was likely but by no means definite.

'Remember, Dad,' she said. 'Pia doesn't name the team until May, so it's not guaranteed.'

'Well, we believe in you, honey,' he replied. 'Whether you do or you don't, we're so proud.'

Alex knew they were proud and that was always her guiding principle – making them as proud as she could, to pay them back and say thank you for all the time and effort they'd put into her dream.

'Perhaps you could have a bit of a rest now, hon?' her mum suggested.

But no. Alex was already looking ahead to the next challenge.

'That's the thing about goals, Mom – you're never really done!' she replied.

The Women's Professional Soccer (WPS) college draft was ahead of her. However, it wasn't without its problems. It was down to six teams and was losing money, with only two sponsors invested in the league.

But it existed. And this meant something. Not just to Alex but to all her teammates and all female American soccer players. It was an issue they regularly discussed. Women's soccer needed a presence and that's what a league gave them.

'I want young girls to turn on the TV and see female players,' said Abby.

'Exactly,' agreed Alex. 'When I watched TV as a kid it was all baseball players and NBA stars.'

Alex thought back to the World Cup in 1999. It

had been so important, not just to her, but to the entire team, who had all once been young girls, dreaming of being soccer players once day. The '99 tournament proved that women could play brilliantly, that they had a place. And that they could make a living from it professionally.

But it couldn't just be about the big tournaments. Women's soccer needed a professional league.

'Men can afford to play badly!' said Abby.

'But we can't!' said Alex.

They laughed, but they knew this was true. There was an extra pressure on them in the league, perhaps one that didn't exist for men. And the more that Alex played, the more she felt as though they had to play their best – not just for their team, but for the next generation of girls who wanted to play soccer. They were the role models now.

Alex felt nervous as she flew to China for the Four Nations Tournament. She was about to find out if she'd been picked for the WPS league. She knew a decision had been made but there was no wi-fi on the plane, so she had to stay patient for a while longer.

She tried to distract herself with movies throughout the flight and listened to her favourite Elvis songs to calm her nerves, but nothing could take her mind off what awaited her.

Her palms were sweating as she walked to baggage reclaim. She soon caught sight of their team's press officer Aaron Heifetz . He had a huge smile on his face. Did this mean good news or was he trying to cushion the fall?

'Alex, good news. You're going to be playing for the Western New York Flash.'

'Oh my! You can't be serious!' It was such a relief for her to hear. Now she was part of a professional league and could play through the winter. This meant she'd be developing all the time, playing with and against her national teammates. If she was chosen for the World Cup team, she'd be in great shape.

CHAPTER 17

WORLD CUP 2011

A few weeks later, Alex was back at the airport.
Her dad laughed as he carried her case through,
preparing to wave her goodbye.

'Oh, man! Even more sweaters!'

'Dad, that's just a suitcase of thermals!' she replied.
Practices for The Flash started that winter and she
would be based in Rochester, New York.

'Get ready for the winters – they're rough!'
warned Abby. 'And it's my hometown – I'm used
to it!'

'Oh yeah,' said Alex, 'practising outdoors is going
to be a big change from California!'

She looked around at all the incredible

international players she would be playing with at The Flash. There were a few friendly, familiar players such as Yael Averbuch, but she couldn't wait to play against stars such as Marta da Silva from Brazil, who she really admired.

Alex's starting salary was a fraction of what a major league baseball rookie would make and there were only a few thousand fans in the stands. Her dad shook his head as he turned to her and said: 'It's not fair, is it.'

Alex agreed, but she knew deep down that she would probably play for less money because she loved the game so much.

'I know, Dad. But this isn't just about me anymore. What's most important is that I do this for all the girls who deserve to have a voice across the world. I don't want to let them down. None of us do.'

Alex went from strength to strength in the team's first season. She scored the first goal in the team's inaugural game against Atlanta Beat and a total of four goals in fourteen games. As many of the players had anticipated, the WPS folded just a year later. But

Alex gave The Flash her all, and helped the team win the last-ever WPS championship.

*

'Have you heard yet?'

'Aww, Dad, you're more nervous than I am...'

'Sorry, honey, we're just, you know, really excited!!'

'Dad, please, I might not get in!'

'Oh, c'mon! You're the last-minute game changer – of course you will! When they need late offence they turn to you!'

'Dad... it's down to all sorts of things, not just one goal. Pia's got to balance out the team, she can't just have ten strikers!'

'Alex, if you're not in the team, I'll shave off my beard!'

She laughed. 'Well, I don't think Pia will care, Dad. But Mom would be pleased!'

Just a week later Alex heard the good news she had been hoping for. She was going to play in the World Cup that summer, in Germany. Her heart swelled with pride and joy as she phoned her parents.

'So Dad, turns out you don't have to shave off your beard!'

'Yay! I knew it!! How exciting!'

'It still feels so surreal – I'm the youngest on the team! But guess what? Christie Rampone is playing! One of my heroes of '99!'

'Amazing! Who else?'

'Abby, Shannon, Hope of course... they're on their third World Cup now. It's a great balance on the team, Dad – we've got Amy who just fights on to the end – and really great defenders like Rachel Buehler... such a good mix of old and new!'

*

There were fifty days to go until Alex left for Germany and she felt as though she would burst with excitement every day. But there was still plenty to do.

Pia had really thought about the best way to use all the team's individual talents. She wanted the players to spend as much as time together in the run-up to the Cup, to ensure they were at their strongest – mentally and physically. When Alex wasn't at camp in Florida, she was flying somewhere else in the country to play for The Flash. However, it was what most of the national team were doing too – leading two separate lives.

'I feel like some rock star on a whirlwind tour of the States!' Alex joked. It was exhausting and there was little time for herself. But she knew the sacrifices were all worth it for the World Cup.

*

Alex stared down at the Number 13 shirt that she wore in Kristine's honour as she prepared to go out onto the pitch. She still couldn't quite believe it as she heard the roar of the crowd of 21,000 in the stadium around her. It was a hot and steamy night in Dresden and Pia had just called Alex in to replace Amy in the seventy-fourth minute. The US team were pretty safe though, leading at 1–0.

'Okay, lucky Number 13,' Alex said to herself, 'it's time to show them what you can do.' She was a little nervous but as Amy approached the sidelines, she couldn't contain her excitement any longer and broke out into a sprint to join her teammates. She thought of her parents cheering her on among the sea of fans, looking down to see her – just a strip of pink darting across the pitch.

She felt as though she was the luckiest person alive. 'I've made it. I'm about to turn twenty-two and I'm playing in the World Cup!' A minute later she watched, spellbound, as Rachel netted a goal past three defenders.

GOAL! As Alex leapt around celebrating with her teammates she thought how happy she was so be on the field to see it. There were tears in her eyes as she hugged Abby.

'This is the best start ever to my World Cup!'

'It's only gonna get better,' said Abby.

In that moment the tournament felt easy. But it wasn't long until they would face one of the toughest and most celebrated teams in the world.

CHAPTER 18

ONE CHANCE

'Okay, guys – I know they're a great side but we've
beaten them twice before – we can do this!'

Pia was relaxed ahead of the USA's quarter-final
game but Alex, along with several members of
the team, didn't quite share her optimism. They
feared Brazil, especially the pint-sized power of
their superstar Marta, who'd won FIFA's Player of
the Year award five years running. Even though the
US had defeated Brazil twice in the Olympics, that
made them even more determined opponents. As
Abby said, with a grimace, 'Boy, have they got a
point to prove because of it. This is not going to
be easy.'

Alex sat on the sidelines and watched the game unfold. She jumped up in the air when, only two minutes into the game, the Brazilians accidentally kicked the ball into their own net – it was an own goal! Both she and Pia shrieked from the sidelines. But almost immediately, Alex sensed the team were going to make them pay for their own mistake. She saw them step up their level of aggressive play, taking four shots on goal in ten minutes. The Brazilian side were more resolute than ever. Alex feared it was only a matter of time, even though the US still had the lead at half-time.

During half-time Pia restated the tactics they needed to work on. 'We can't give any stupid fouls,' she warned. 'They will dive for balls and claw their way back. We need to control the tempo of the game, and we need to keep the ball!'

'I've got my work cut out for me with Marta!' said Rachel in defence.

'I know, and you're doing a great job.'

But they couldn't have anticipated just how bad things were going to get. Events took an unexpected turn in the second half when Rachel was given a red card for fouling Marta.

'What?!' Alex shook her head in disbelief at the sidelines. How could her teammate be sent off?

They were now ten players down and Brazil had a penalty. Alex groaned as she saw Marta step up to take it. Marta was Brazil's penalty queen. She took the shot and it effortlessly sailed in past Hope. Alex could feel the pressure pile on as she waited for her chance to make a difference.

In the seventy-second minute, Alex was called on. She was thrilled to get out there, but was immediately struck by how menacing the atmosphere felt. She took a deep breath and vowed to play her best. But as regulation time drew to a close, they were still tied. Now, the challenge was to prepare for extra time. 'Here we go,' thought Alex.

The chants of 'Team USA! Team USA!' rose up from the crowd. They were right behind them in their toughest match yet. But it was Marta, the Brazilian superstar, who was to score again first.

By the ninety-second minute, Brazil led by 2–1.

With only ten players on the pitch, the match was only going to get harder, but Alex felt each and every one of them double their effort for the next half hour.

She heard her teammates shout to each other: 'Don't give up!' and 'It ain't over till the whistle blows!' But as they neared the end of extra time the score remained the same: 2–1. The chants of 'USA! USA!' were practically making the stands shake.

The US team had just three minutes to make a difference. Alex looked over at Abby, who they always turned to for leadership in the toughest of situations. She saw her pointing up with one finger, as though she was directing to the sky. Alex realised she was signalling the number one.

She started to scream: 'One chance! One moment! That's all it takes! All it takes is one chance!'

It suddenly seemed so simple. Anything could change in an instant. They just had to believe. With barely a minute to spare, Megan got hold of the ball and tore down the field, running faster than Alex had ever seen her run. She kicked far from behind the penalty box. At the crucial moment, and with

perfect timing, Abby jumped up in the air next to
two defenders. The ball made contact with her head
and everyone watched, as it sailed into the goal.

GOAL!!!

'Whoop! Abby! You've done it!' They had tied
2–2. Now they faced a penalty shoot-out. But Abby's
beautiful goal had raised their spirits and they felt as
though they could do anything.

'The momentum is with us now!' said Abby.

The team huddled together in solidarity and
watched as five of their players stepped forward to
take penalties – Alex held her breath each time
and marvelled as Shannon, Carli, Abby, Megan and
Alex Krieger netted each shot into the goal. It had
been a rollercoaster ride but they were through to
the semi-finals.

After the game, Pia gathered the team together to
congratulate them all on keeping their cool.

'I'm so proud of you all,' she said. 'You didn't let
losing Rachel rattle you. You pulled through and
didn't let it affect your concentration on the pitch.'

'There were some really unfair decisions in there,

but we kept calm and carried on,' said Abby.

It was a lesson to them all. They knew they had to keep a level head when dealing with any tough situation they encountered during a game, however unfair it seemed.

CHAPTER 19

LIVE YOUR GOALS

Next, the USA faced France. As Alex had learnt from playing many different nationalities, each national team had their own particular style and skill.

'I'm afraid their soccer is just as good as their food,' warned Pia of the French, 'perhaps better. They're very precise and have incredible finesse. But, we have that too.'

'Plus power, fitness and speed!' cried Megan.

'Yeah, and we've got Baby Horse!' they all laughed, and Alex blushed. She was yet to wear out this nickname and wondered if she would always feel a little like the baby of the pack. She was proud, though. She knew her energy, which she brought to the pitch when she was brought on in the second half, boosted the team.

'What a stride!'

'There's no stopping her when she gallops across the field!'

They continued to tease Alex, but then Abby looked her in the eye and said in a serious tone: 'You just need one opportunity, just one.'

Alex knew she was right and she hoped she would have her chance that night to prove it. She looked down at the 'Live Your Goals' sponsorship slogan on her US strip. The campaign had been launched by the FAI (Football Association of Ireland) in conjunction with FIFA to introduce more females to the game. She was doing this for them as well.

It was a cooler night out on the pitch in Frankfurt. France were indeed a strong side. Despite midfielder Lauren Cheney scoring in the ninth minute the opposition put a lot of pressure on the defenders. Plus, the US were still missing Rachel's defence, although Becky Sauerbrunn replaced her. Hope was also performing some incredible saves, but Alex knew they couldn't get complacent.

At half-time, Pia ran through their tactics. 'We need to keep up on our defence – they're doing everything they can to push through.'

'But it's okay 'cause we've got Hope!' rallied Abby.

'You're proving you're the best in the sport today, Hope, that's for sure,' said Pia.

They all agreed. But ten minutes into the second half, even Hope couldn't save an incredible shot from the French side.

At that moment Pia decided to send Alex into the match earlier than scheduled: 'Okay, it's your turn now,' and added, 'Push, run like crazy, control the ball.'

Alex was happy that Pia had sent her in earlier to give the players more opportunities to score.

Pia's strategy worked for the team. But deep down, Alex desperately wanted to score a goal. She smiled to herself as she admitted: 'I want to show the world I'm more than just Baby Horse.'

Alex felt the determined mood of the team as

soon as she arrived on the field. But she also felt the determination of several defenders marking her, who were hot on her heels.

The second half remained scoreless until the seventy-ninth minute. It was Abby's turn to strike a magnificent header after Lauren took a corner kick.

GOAL!!! They were 2–1 up! And Abby had just become the joint top scorer of all-time in the Women's World Cup finals. The mood was buoyant.

France continued to push hard on their attack. But three minutes later, Alex saw an opportunity as she waited down the field on the left wing. Her time came when Megan picked up the ball and jabbed it to her on the left side. She caught it on first touch. She was through, heading towards the penalty box. She tore past four defenders, and sped down the flank away from one who had been hot on her heels. She was on her own and in the penalty box. As she approached the goalkeeper, she saw her confusion. She heard her dad's voice in her head talking her through the motions – 'Take the ball to the goal, now, where do you want it to go? Aim! Finish it,

Alex! Then we can have ice cream.' She thought of her mum and dad, both up there. Rooting for her. In every single game.

Alex saw the goalkeeper slide to the ground, wrongly anticipating the timing of her shot. And she saw her moment. 'Shoot!'

She slammed the ball with her left foot right over the goalkeeper's head. Everything slowed down as she saw it sail through the air. As it hit the back of the net she heard a giant swoosh sound. A cool and calm feeling of certainty overcame her. She'd known all along she could do it. And she'd been working up to it all those years, since she was a little girl. Her first World Cup goal.

She heard the crowd go wild. She felt Megan leap on her as she ran back down the field. She saw Abby run towards her.

'You did it, Alex! You did it! See?! Big things can happen in just one moment.'

'You're not Baby Horse now, Alex!' cried Megan.

They had done it. Now they were on their way to Frankfurt in the final against Japan.

CHAPTER 20

WORLD CUP TENSION

'This is one of the biggest games of your careers,' said Pia, but no-one in the US team needed the reminder.

It was twelve years since the USA had made it to a World Cup final, let alone won one. They all felt as though they'd worked so hard and overcome too much in this tournament to lose now.

But although they were determined to win, their hearts went out to the Japanese team too. Earlier that year, Japan had been hit by a devastating earthquake and tsunami that had killed 15,000 people. The country was still reeling. The success of their women's football team in the tournament was a positive news story in a year that had been overshadowed by tragedy. The US team had a lot of respect for them.

Pia gathered them together before the game. 'They are a technical and precise team,' she said of their opponents. 'And though we may be better I think we all understand this doesn't mean they can't win.'

They'd learnt this lesson only too well in their Mexico match. But still, they believed they had a chance to win the title – just as their heroes had, back in '99.

'Okay, guys!' rallied Abby. 'Let's bring this title home! This is our year!'

As the team filed out onto the field in front of a cheering crowd of 48,000 at Commerzbank-Arena, Alex's heart swelled with pride and joy. All she could see was wave upon wave of star spangled banners.

Somewhere among them all her family was watching. She thought of all her friends watching back home and the hundreds of supportive messages she'd received. Some were from teachers and old teammates she'd not seen in years – they were all behind her, willing her on.

She realised she'd never played in front of so many people. It was everything she'd ever worked for and although she shook with nerves she reminded herself to stay focused on the team and not herself. As she watched from the sidelines she could see that both teams were on fire, playing their absolute hearts out. She gasped in amazement at Megan's long passes and Abby's shots on target. But at half-time, the game was scoreless.

As they walked back onto the field for the second half, Alex felt the pressure mount. Their country was relying on them. Something had to happen in the next forty-five minutes. 'Remember how competitive you are, Alex,' she told herself as she focused on the game and put to one side the traumas that Japan had suffered. 'This is a competition, after all!'

In the forty-ninth minute Alex saw a chance. She charged into the penalty area and picked up a cross from Heather. She shot. BOOM! It smacked the post. Alex threw her arms up in frustration.

Twenty minutes later Abby almost got a header in but it soared over the bar. They could all feel the tension mount. They were almost seventy minutes into regulation and had taken so many more shots than the opposition. When would they score?

Anything can happen, Alex reminded herself: 'It only takes a minute. Don't give up yet.'

It was the sixty-ninth minute. Alex was in midfield waiting for an opportunity. She could see a scramble for the ball in the penalty area between four US players and one opponent. Then she saw the ball come soaring down the pitch towards her. Megan had taken an incredibly long and precise shot, more than fifty yards away from her. The ball landed a little to her left and began to roll away fast.

Alex charged after it, unaware of the Japanese defender desperate to chase her down. As she made contact with the ball, she dribbled it for a few seconds with her right foot before lining it up with her left boot. BOOM! She saw it soar through the air and land in the top right of the net. It was a perfect finish!

GOAL!!!

Alex fell to the ground with relief and joy. As Abby was the first teammate to run towards her, she wondered for a moment if she was dreaming . Had she really just scored the first goal in the World Cup final? She heard the crowd explode and it dawned on her. This was real. All the coaches and teammates she'd worked with, all the extra training and drills flashed before her. Every drop of sweat and tears had been worth it for this one moment of pure, blissful happiness. The team fell about her whooping and cheering. She wished that they could carry on celebrating forever.

But no. It wasn't over yet.

'Come on guys – we got a game to play!'

They still had twenty minutes to play and as they scrambled back to the centre of the field they were about to discover, yet again, just how quickly events could turn around. In the eightieth minute Japan levelled. With ten minutes of regulation time to go Alex felt their energy drop. It was their second extra time in three games and they were tired.

Now, more than ever, they needed to hang on to their determination to win.

The connection between Abby and Alex was as close as ever, though. Neither forward gave up. They looked all set to achieve their dream of winning when Alex nailed a perfect pass to Abby in the penalty box. She headed the ball straight in.

GOAL!!!

They just needed to hang on for the next fifteen minutes of overtime.

Alex glanced nervously at the clock, wishing the minutes away. But in the 117th minute, Japan took a corner kick that led them to tie again – 2–2. It was time for the dreaded penalties.

The team huddled together as they watched each player from both sides take their turn. Alex watched in disbelief as three US players missed their shots, all in a row. She felt Megan grip her hand. They normally found penalties so easy, but the pressure was clearly getting to them all – and the opposition had only missed one penalty.

Abby was out next. If she missed it they were out.

But she stepped up and effortlessly nailed it into the net. She ran back and gave everyone a look that said: 'It's not over yet.'

Hope needed time to collect herself for the next shot. If the next shot went in, Japan would win. The US team watched in dismay as the next player kicked the ball, sailing it perfectly over Hope's head.

Then they heard the opposition begin to scream and the sidelined players run onto the pitch. It was all over.

Alex walked slowly to the stands where her parents, her sister Jeri and her aunt were waiting for her. As soon as she saw their faces she burst into tears. They hugged her and offered as much comfort as they could but there was little they could say. Alex and the team had worked so hard to get to the final but she couldn't help but churn over some of the mistakes they'd made and missed opportunities throughout the game. She knew she would still be processing them over the next few weeks.

Pia tried to comfort them afterwards. 'Please don't

blame yourselves. It's useless and it will get you nowhere.'

The team decided there and then: 'We'll learn from this. And we'll be back.'

CHAPTER 21

2012

'Oh my God! Listen to this! From Barack Obama!'

Abby read out a tweet to the rest of the team:

'I couldn't be prouder of the women of the US national team after a hard-fought game.'

'No way!'

The emotional pain of losing was lessened by the incredible support they had received from the press and from fans. Their fans acknowledged that they'd all fought as hard as they could.

'You played as a team, honey,' said her dad. 'Each and every one of you contributed to those incredible goals.'

He added: 'And you? Two World Cup goals and

an assist? You're no longer just Baby Horse, are you?
You showed incredible maturity out there.'

She laughed. 'No, Dad.' She'd proved that she
wasn't just some twenty-two-year-old fresh out of
college.

'When you do win, and you will next time, it's
going to feel all the sweeter because of this defeat.'

'Thanks, Dad.'

'And it's the Olympics next year – don't forget
that!'

There were many events to help take Alex's
mind off the next World Cup. It was also clear
that their performance in the final had increased
attendance figures at WPS games. In Western
New York Flash's championship game against
Philadelphia Independence there were more than
10,000 spectators. This may have been a fraction
of the number at a World Cup final, but it was a
record for a WPS final. They all knew this
was a positive sign that times were changing and
that the world was beginning to take women's
soccer more seriously.

Western New York Flash played for 104 minutes before it went into overtime and penalties. Alex laughed to herself as she thought: 'This seems to be the theme of my life at the moment!' But this time she could heave a sigh of relief as the Western New York Flash went on to win the Championship.

*

'We kind of knew this was coming, didn't we?' said one of Alex's teammates.

'Yeah, it still sucks,' said another.

'Why does it keep happening?' wondered a third.

Alex looked around at her teammates' bitterly disappointed faces, and wished she could answer that question. They'd just received the news that the WPS had folded. This was the second women's soccer league to shut down and yet again, they were all wondering about the future of the game.

Alex decided, there and then, that she'd do all she could to advance professional soccer for women. She vowed: 'I'm going to play to the absolute highest standard that I can. The more exciting the games are, the more people will attend and the more money they'll plough in.'

There was already a silver lining to the WPS folding. Alex was offered a place at Sounders, a semi-professional team based in Seattle, which meant a reunion; some of her friends from the national team also played for them – Hope, Megan, Stephanie and Sydney.

They all greeted her at the airport: 'Baby Horse!!!'

She fell into their arms. 'I've missed you all so much!'

It felt so great to play together as a team again and to sort out some of the problems that had held them back at the World Cup.

It was the perfect warm-up for their next big challenge – the 2012 Olympics in London. They were all beginning to get excited about the qualifiers. But Alex also had a personal goal in mind. This time she didn't want to just be a late-game weapon. She wanted to be included in the starter roster on at least one of the qualifying games.

*

After yet another win in the qualifiers, Pia told the team, 'If you keep playing like this, I think there's a good chance you'll win the Olympics.'

Alex believed this too. They were all buzzing from their performances and she felt as though they were playing some of the best games of their lives – their defence was stronger than ever and they were a scoring machine, beating the Dominican Republic 14–0 and Guatemala 13–0.

Alex felt incredibly proud to be amongst such a powerhouse of players. But she knew there were still no guarantees she'd be included in the starter roster, so she worked as hard as she could, to prove she was ready throughout the tournament.

That evening before their qualifier final against Canada, Pia drew Alex aside. 'You've worked incredibly hard and I'm so proud of all you've done.'

She pulled out the starting roster line-up. Alex broke out into a huge smile as she saw her name on the list.

'You more than deserve it,' said Pia.

Alex went out onto the field on a high that night, more determined than ever to show Pia she'd made the right decision.

Alex and Abby were both upfront as strikers in a 4–4–2 formation. The chemistry between the pair was undeniable as they led the team in a 4–0 victory over their rivals.

Pia congratulated them all after the win. 'You all did such an amazing job.'

Then she turned to Abby and Alex. 'You've always played well together,' she said, 'but that was something else today. The connection you have is incredible. Keep playing like this and we can win the Olympics!'

Alex turned to Abby. 'You've taught me so much. Thank you.'

'And there's always more to learn,' Abby replied with a smile. 'Our work's not finished yet.'

*

The US team boarded the flight to Heathrow Airport: 'London – here we come!'

Abby was busy impersonating the English accent. 'Would anyone like a cup of tea?' Everyone turned to her and groaned.

'Abby – that is awful!'

'The English sound so much cuter than that!'

'So do their football clubs,' said Alex. 'Arsenal, Tottenham, Chelsea. And their leagues are so big they're even followed internationally!'

'I already think these guys are the bomb if they love their soccer so much,' said Abby. 'Even if they do like that weird drink, tea.'

'Abby, they call it football there! Football!'

Alex felt so happy as they flew to London. She was thrilled to have the opportunity to play in a country where the game was so important. She'd already had a great summer, playing brilliantly in both the Algarve Cup and Sweden Invitational. With a total of seventeen goals that season, she'd become the US team's leading scorer. She felt confident she could help the team to Olympic gold victory next.

But as she looked over to Abby, she remembered

her words. There was a lot of work ahead of them. Japan and Canada (who had won the Algarve Cup) would be tough to beat. But Alex was more than ready. And she believed the whole team deserved to win.

CHAPTER 22

THEATRE OF DREAMS

'Old Traffoooord.'

Megan kept repeating the words in an extremely posh English voice as the team headed out to the historic stadium to play Canada, where nearly 27,000 spectators were waiting for them. The team chattered excitedly as chants of 'USA! USA!' reverberated around the stadium.

'Well, I guess it is pretty old.'

'Everything's old here – this place is probably older than the oldest house in the States.'

'Do you know what its nickname is?'

'Theatre of Dreams.'

'Wow, if stadiums could speak.'

They were silent for a moment as they marvelled at the thought of the famous matches and players the stadium had seen – from Best to Beckham. Now it was their turn to make history there. They continued to joke and make fun of each other's English accents. But they all knew how important this game was. If they beat Canada they would take on Japan in the final.

The Olympics hadn't been the easiest tournament so far. They'd had a rocky start with France, met with an aggressive Colombian team – one team member had punched Abby – and a tough game against New Zealand, where Alex had been knocked to the ground so hard she'd been checked over by a medic.

But here they were, ready for Canada. And as Pia said of her team before they played: 'They like the pressure. The harder the game, the more you get out of the team.' However, they could never have anticipated just how much pressure Canada was about to put them under.

From the start it was clear that Canada was

playing aggressively. Within ten minutes of kick-off, a defender had hit Alex on the shoulder and knocked her off her feet. Her teammates looked on with shock and surprise. The US had a fight on their hands. They concentrated on keeping the pressure on in midfield, determined not to let any balls reach Hope down in goal.

But after twenty-one minutes, Canada's aggressive play paid off as they scored their first goal. Ten minutes later, Alex attempted a header when the ball came her way after a free kick.

'Darn it!' cried Alex, when it went wide of the goal. Headers weren't her strength, but she knew she had to take every opportunity in the match. When the whistle blew for half-time, Canada were 1–0 up.

Pia gathered the dejected-looking team together. She looked them all in the eye as she said:

'You've made some great play, girls, you've had possession of the ball 55 per cent of the time and I think overall you're playing better. I think you can win this! No, I *know* you can win this!'

Alex believed this in her heart too. They had forty-five more minutes to make a difference. All it would take was one moment, one opportunity.

They left the locker room feeling pumped up and raring to go.

'We've got this!'

But the Canadians continued to fight a tough game. Alex looked over at Abby with concern. She was taking quite a beating from the opposition – at one point she was knocked to the ground and then sandwiched between two players.

But in the fifty-fourth minute the team had a breakthrough. Megan Rapinoe took a corner kick that sailed through the air. Alex watched in amazement as she saw a huddle of white Canadian shirts attempt to block it. But it was too perfect a shot. There was nothing they could do as it landed right inside the near corner of the goal.

GOAL!!! An Olympic goal, no less – straight from the kick to the net. Was it the wind? Luck? Terrific spin? It didn't matter as the team fell about hugging and laughing. They had tied. And they felt as though they were properly back in the game.

But in the sixty-sixth minute Canada stepped it up a gear when Christine Sinclair scored her second goal of the match with a header.

In that instant, Alex felt the determination of her team soar. Just three minutes later it paid off when Megan shot one of the most astonishing kicks Alex had ever seen her take. Both sides watched in amazement as the ball flew seventy feet through the air and into the goal. The score was now 2–2!

Now the pressure was on to get ahead. But neither side was giving up. Canada's Christine Sinclair scored yet again with a corner kick. Then Abby took a penalty for the USA – BOOM. It went straight in. When would this be over? There was still ten minutes to go, a long time in soccer.

At ninety minutes, Alex felt the team's energy ebbing. She got a chance to take the ball down the field past a defender. She passed to Abby who kicked it wide and then fell to the ground, slapping her hands against her forehead in frustration. Even the calmest players who always held it together were feeling the strain.

'Don't give up,' Alex said to herself, 'keep trying, keep pushing.' No-one wanted a penalty shoot-out and there had never been one in Olympic women's soccer.

Extra time started, but neither side relented. Alex could hear every player breathing heavily, as they ran furiously up and down the field. They were all feeling the pressure.

Before the final fifteen minutes Abby huddled the US team all together. 'Everybody needs to believe in each other right now. And keep it together. Believe we're going to win. We're going to do it if we play as a team.'

But as the physical and mental pressures began to mount up, it was difficult for Alex to focus and believe in her own motivational words. She could feel old aches and pains returning, and she desperately needed some water.

As she felt her spirit begin to flag, she fell to the ground. A player had collided into her. She wanted to lie there for the rest of the game. But then she thought of her parents up in the stands watching.

'Get up Alex and make them proud,' she told herself. 'Get up and win this game once and for all.' And as she got to her feet she thought: 'This game is still ours. We've made great passes. We're the better side.'

She knew that everyone else was contemplating penalties, though. She could see it in their faces.

'No,' she thought, 'it's not going to end that way.' At 120 minutes, three minutes of stoppage time were added. Alex vowed to keep fighting.

With just forty-five seconds left in the game, Alex was in the penalty area among a swarm of white jerseys. She saw Heather O'Reilly run hard at the ball with one last ounce of strength left in her. She crossed it perfectly towards the goal.

'C'mon Alex, here's your chance,' she thought. 'Forget the headers you've missed before. Forget the coaches who have said they're not "your strength". Do this. Connect!'

Alex jumped and felt the ball against her head. 'Shoot!!!' And then she heard a roar from the crowd so loud that there was no mistake. It was as if every person in the Theatre of Dreams had stood up on cue and was screaming for joy, with every part of their soul.

GOAL!!!

No penalty shoot-out. The USA had done it. They'd won the game.

Alex felt the tears begin to well up in her eyes as the team hugged and squeezed her with the last little bits of energy they had in them. She heard Abby's voice shouting in her ear: 'I love you! You just sent us to the gold-medal game!'

Alex burst into tears. It had been a long, exhausting game. She couldn't believe that her header, usually one of her weaknesses, had taken them into the finals.

CHAPTER 23

GOING FOR GOLD

'Morgan's miracle!' Alex's match-saving goal in the final seconds of the USA's game against Canada was heralded for days after. But Alex knew it was no miracle. It's what she had been training for her whole life. Years of hard work had taken her up to that goal.

And so to the Olympic final against Japan at Wembley Stadium, the second-largest stadium in all of Europe. As Alex walked out on to the pitch the noise of 80,000 people cheering was almost deafening. The enormity of the team's achievement hit home again. There was no way a women's soccer team would have filled a stadium of that size

years before. But she was part of a team who had
continually proven itself and she knew they deserved
this audience. The crowd had responded to their
incredible play.

It had been one year and twenty-three days since
Japan had beaten the USA at the World Cup. Alex
knew they were all determined to set the record
straight.

But she knew Japan were determined as well.
They wanted to prove that it was no fluke they were
in the Olympic final. Homare Sawa, the brilliant
forward who had scored consistently throughout the
World Cup four years before, was in this year's team.
The US knew they had their work cut out for them
in counter-attacking her technical genius.

As the whistle blew for the start of the final, the
USA were reminded once again of Japan's disciplined
style of play. But within ten minutes the US had
scored, with Alex and Abby assisting on a goal for
Carli Lloyd.

In goal, Hope had her work cut out for her.
She saved goal after goal, jumping in the air with

incredible strength and determination. Alex watched her skill in amazement.

By half-time the US were still 1–0 up. There was no time for complacency, but even with such tough opponents, their dream of winning gold looked like becoming reality when Carli scored her second goal of the match – a beautiful long pass from behind the penalty line.

Surely Japan couldn't claw back now with only thirty-five minutes to go? But as they all knew, it only took one moment for everything to change. And it did. In the sixty-third minute, Japan's valiant play got a result. Hope saved a ball from Sawa but it deflected back to her. She nudged it to striker Yuki Ogimi who scored.

Alex saw Pia looking anxious in the stands. Could Japan beat them again? Memories of the 2011 World Cup came flooding back to her. Could this be a repeat performance? 'No,' Alex silently resolved, 'we are going to win.'

In the seventy-fourth minute, Alex got hold of the ball and took it down the field. She took a shot that went nowhere near the goal. 'Oh Alex,' she berated herself, 'you should have passed to Abby!' She was cross with her mistake but vowed not to dwell on it.

In the eighty-second minute, they all breathed a huge sigh of relief as Hope made another spectacular save – it was later heralded as 'the save heard round the world'. Once again, Alex thanked her lucky stars she was able to see it first-hand.

Alex glanced at the clock. There were eight minutes to go. The US were safe. For now.

'USA!!! USA!!!' The chants grew even louder and the Wembley stands shook even harder. As ninety minutes approached, two minutes of stoppage time were added. Surely it was nearly over?

'Two minutes to gold,' Alex told herself. 'Two minutes.'

She held her breath, wishing the seconds would speed away. Then, finally, the whistle blew. The relief washed over her as she nearly fell to the ground with exhaustion.

They'd done it!!! They'd survived the weeks of hard work and tough-tackling players on the pitch –

the team held each other tight and tears of joy ran down their faces as all the tension lifted from their shoulders.

As the medal ceremony began, the victors beamed from ear to ear, in a state of disbelief and joy. Canada came out first to claim bronze, followed by silver medallists Japan. Finally, as their stars-and-stripes flag was raised, the American team sang their hearts out to the national anthem.

Alex felt incredibly proud of the team as the gold medal was slipped around her neck. They had all played a huge part in making this dream come true. It was, without doubt, the greatest achievement of her life.

After the match the girls were interviewed by the press.

'How does it feel to win?'

'Absolutely amazing!' they replied. 'But it's been a tough few weeks – we just want to celebrate!'

Now was the time to let their hair down and bask in their victory.

The team celebrated into the early hours. They'd

not had much chance to enjoy the sights of London but now the city seemed even more beautiful, as they saw the first rays of sunrise light up St Paul's Cathedral and the London Eye.

For Alex, though, the best part of the celebrations was spending time with her entire family. Finally, at 6:30am, her parents dropped her off at the Olympic village. She collapsed into bed, just about ready for sleep, with the sounds of the jubilant crowd still ringing in her ears and the overjoyed faces of her parents, sisters and teammates in her mind. She fell into a deep sleep, still clutching the gold medal tight in her hands.

The next thing she knew, her phone was ringing. The Olympic win still felt like a dream but her dad's voice brought her back to earth.

'Honey – guess what?! I missed my flight home!'

'Oh no! How?'

'Well, on the underground train your mom and I went all the way to the end of the Piccadilly line and back!'

'You were only supposed to go to Heathrow!'

'Yeah... we fell asleep!'

'Oh, Dad – I'm sorry!'

'Alex, it was hysterical – I don't know what the poor ticket collector thought we'd been up to – crashing out on the subway like that at our age!'

Alex started to laugh.

'It was worth it,' he continued. 'I'd do it all over again to see you win gold – one of the best nights of my life.'

'Oh, Dad!' Alex began to cry all over again.

*

The year 2012 had been one of the best of Alex's life and she didn't believe it could get any better. But it did – at the end of the year, she was named US Soccer's 2012 Female Athlete of the Year, a prize voted on by the fans, media and soccer representatives, as well as taking third place in the FIFA Ballon d'Or. She also joined Mia Hamm as the only American woman to have scored twenty goals and twenty assists in the same calendar year.

Alex was at the height of her game and couldn't wait to find out what the next few years held.

CHAPTER 24

THE HOMECOMING

'Alex!' 'Alex!'

Alex was one of three US national team players to join Portland Thorns, and a crowd of fans jostled for her attention as she made her way into the stand. It was their first game of their inaugural season against Seattle Reign. She remembered her dad saying, 'You should always be the last person signing autographs.' And she made sure that she was, making time for every single girl who wanted to ask questions; it had always been so important to her when she was little.

'How do I get to be a soccer star, Alex?' asked one young fan.

'Work hard,' she began, 'always do more than your opponent and don't give up! And remember – dreams can come true!'

'Can I have your hairband please?'

'Woah! I don't know about that!' she laughed as she touched the pink accessory that so many of her fans now sported. It had become such an important part of her signature look.

*

Alex loved playing with the Portland Thorns. She was reunited with a couple of her national teammates – Rachel Buehler and Tobin Heath.

She was also playing alongside her previous rival: Christine Sinclair from Canada.

'Ha!' They both laughed and joked together, 'We're on the same team so we gotta be nice to each other now!'

But what really made Alex's heart soar was the sheer number of people watching the games. Women's soccer was now attracting crowds of 17,000.

'Maybe a professional soccer league is going to work in the United States,' she thought. The

National Women's Soccer League (NWSL) was still in its infancy, but Alex was more confident now than ever that women's soccer was getting the respect and audiences it deserved.

Her dad laughed when Alex told him NWSL tournaments would be shown on ESPN and Fox Sports. 'Now I can watch you on the screen, I don't have to come to every game.' Of course, he still made it to every game, though.

Alex did miss her great friend Abby who'd moved back to New York, and Megan who'd moved to France to play. But both players offered encouraging words.

'Hey, don't worry Alex,' they said. 'It'll be the World Cup before you know it and we'll be back as a team soon! The best team in the world!'

And they were right. Despite the US team's Olympic triumph in 2012, the World Cup remained at the forefront of Alex's mind. And in 2015, after the disappointments in 2011, she longed for the team to win.

*

Alex urgently needed reassurance, and her dear old friend Abby provided it: 'Don't worry, Alex. Remember when I broke my leg? I went on to play even better than ever.'

Alex had just found out she had plica syndrome. The soft tissue on the area of her knee bone was inflamed and was causing excruciating pain. She feared the worst. What if she couldn't play in the World Cup? As she looked into the faces of her teammates she felt crushed at the thought of not being able to play with them.

She had two choices – take four weeks off and hope it repaired itself, or have surgery to remove the piece of soft tissue that was causing the issue. Alex chose to rest but this meant missing several friendly games. She kept on practising and going to rehab. But the press wanted to know whether or not she'd be able to play.

Alex knew she couldn't push her body and that it would give up if she did. But she was desperate to play.

The team's new coach, Jill Ellis, was quick to

reassure her. 'You're young. You're healthy. And you're going to help us win the World Cup. I know it.'

'I don't care if I never walk again! I just want this chance, Jill!'

Alex thought back sixteen years to 1999, watching Mia Hamm and her heroes, the last time that the US women's team had claimed the title.

Jill smiled. 'It won't come to that, Alex. You are going to get through this.'

*

Alex was about to walk out onto the soccer field at Winnipeg in Canada. She was about to play the first game of the 2015 World Cup against Australia.

Abby squeezed her hand, and said, 'You've made it.'

Alex looked back at her and smiled. She knew this would be an emotional tournament for her too, as she'd decided it would be her last World Cup.

She breathed a huge sigh of relief. She'd practised every day in Canada and her plica was no longer bothering her. But she also knew she wasn't quite the same player as she had been, and she couldn't remember the last time she'd played a full ninety minutes.

The press were calling her the 'face of the US Women's National Team', so it was difficult not to feel the pressure. But as she walked out onto the pitch, hand-in-hand with the youth player, she broke out in a smile from ear to ear.

Right there and then she decided: 'I'm just going to play the sport I love and do it with joy.'

The US team made it to the final, where they beat Japan decisively in a 5–2 victory. The match was watched by 27.7 million Americans, which made it the most watched soccer game – men's or women's – in history. When the referee blew the whistle the team ran on to the pitch and jumped up and down hugging each other in a circle, tears streaming down their faces.

Alex knew she'd never been happier before – not even when she'd scored during the U-20 World Cup or got her first call-up to the national team. This was what she'd worked for her entire life, ever since she'd watched Julie Foudy, Brandi Chastain and Mia

Hamm from her home in Diamond Bar. And best
of all, she was sharing it with the best team in the
world.

*

'We are delighted to welcome home, not only a hero
to the city, but a national star.'

Alex had returned home to Diamond Bar for a
special ceremony to receive the first ever key to
the city – an honour presented by the city council
to an individual who has achieved incredible
accomplishments.

She looked around at the large crowd that
had gathered to greet her in Pantera Park. It was
difficult to hold back the tears as she recalled all the
wonderful, long summer evenings she'd spent there,
practising soccer with her dad. She steadied herself
before she spoke:

'It's really amazing to be part of a community that
supports each other; a community that I feel so
much a part of. I have this remembrance forever,
which means I'll always have a piece of Diamond
Bar with me.'

MORGAN HONOURS

Western New York Flash
🏆 WPS Championship: 2011

Portland Thorns FC
🏆 NWSL Championship: 2013

Lyon
🏆 Division 1 Féminine: 2017
🏆 Coupe de France Féminine: 2017
🏆 UEFA Women's Champions League: 2017

International
🏆 Olympic Gold Medal: 2012

🏆 FIFA Women's World Cup: 2015, Runner-up: 2011

🏆 FIFA U-20 Women's World Cup: 2008

🏆 Algarve Cup: 2011, 2013, 2015

🏆 Four Nations Tournament: 2011

🏆 SheBelieves Cup: 2016, 2018

🏆 CONCACAF Women's Championship: 2014, 2018

🏆 CONCACAF Women's Olympic Qualifying

🏆 Tournament: 2012, 2016

🏆 ESPY Award Best Team: 2015

Individual

🏆 FIFA U-20 Women's World Cup Silver Ball: 2008

🏆 ESPY Award Best Breakthrough Athlete nominee: 2012

🏆 ESPY Award Best Moment Nominee: 2013

🏆 Women's Sports Foundation Sportswoman of the Year, Team Sport: 2012

🏆 US Soccer Athlete of the Year: 2012, 2018

🏆 FIFA World Player of the Year finalist: 2012

🏆 National Women's Soccer League Second Best XI: 2013, 2017

🏆 CONCACAF Player of the Year: 2013, 2016, 2017, 2018

🏆 USWNT All-Time Best XI: 2013

🏆 SheBelieves Cup Golden Ball and MVP: 2016[

🏆 FIFPro: FIFPro World XI 2016, 2017

🏆 CONCACAF Women's Championship golden boot: 2018

🏆 Concacaf's Female Player of the Year: 2013, 2016, 2017, 2018

🏆 US Soccer Female Player of the Year: 2012, 2018

🏆 FIFA Women's World Player of the Year finalist: 2012

MORGAN

(10) **THE FACTS**

NAME: Alexandra Patricia Morgan Carrasco

DATE OF BIRTH: 2 July 1989

AGE: 29

PLACE OF BIRTH: San Dimas, California, United States

NATIONALITY: American

POSITION: Striker

THE STATS

Height (cm):	**170**
Club appearances:	**127**
Club goals:	**59**
Club trophies:	**5**
International appearances:	**165**
International goals:	**103**
International trophies:	**1**
Ballon d'Ors:	**0**

★ ★ ★ **HERO RATING: 90** ★ ★ ★

GREATEST MOMENTS

Type and search the web links to see the magic for yourself!

13 JULY 2011: FIFA WOMEN'S WORLD CUP UNITED STATES V FRANCE 3–1, BORUSSIA-PARK, MÖNCHENGLADBACH

https://www.youtube.com/watch?v=GFk1w6Picks
Alex scores her first World Cup goal in the eighty-third minute, taking the team through to a secure 3–1 victory. It confirms her reputation as a late game threat to be reckoned with, as well as her transformation as she grows out of her nickname, 'Baby Horse'.

17 JULY 2011: FIFA WOMEN'S WORLD CUP UNITED STATES V JAPAN 2–2, COMMERZBANK-ARENA, FRANKFURT

https://www.youtube.com/watch?v=waLFeW3aHgQ

Almost seventy minutes into the match, with both sides yet to score, Alex finally breaks the deadlock, and scores the first goal of the final. It wasn't to be, for the US side, though, who went on to lose out to Japan on penalties.

6 AUGUST 2012: OLYMPICS CANADA V UNITED STATES 3–4, OLD TRAFFORD, MANCHESTER

https://www.youtube.com/watch?v=8TTVF3_3JBU

Alex scores just twelve seconds into the game with a right-footed volley. Her goal is believed to be the fastest scored in US history. The match was the team's first competitive game since winning the World Cup in 2015.

10 FEBRUARY 2016: CONCACAF WOMEN'S OLYMPIC QUALIFYING TOURNAMENT UNITED STATES V COSTA RICA 5–0, TOYOTA STADIUM, TEXAS

https://www.youtube.com/watch?v=dciJVn-04Gs

Alex scores just twelve seconds into the game with a right-footed volley. Her goal is believed to be the fastest scored in US history. The match was the team's first competitive game since winning the World Cup in 2015.

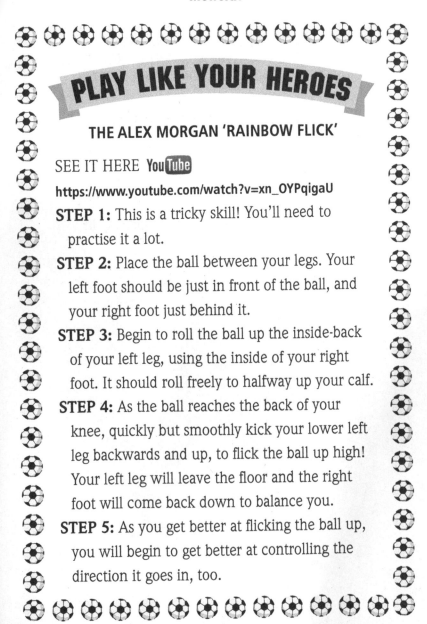

PLAY LIKE YOUR HEROES

THE ALEX MORGAN 'RAINBOW FLICK'

SEE IT HERE You Tube

https://www.youtube.com/watch?v=xn_OYPqigaU

STEP 1: This is a tricky skill! You'll need to practise it a lot.

STEP 2: Place the ball between your legs. Your left foot should be just in front of the ball, and your right foot just behind it.

STEP 3: Begin to roll the ball up the inside-back of your left leg, using the inside of your right foot. It should roll freely to halfway up your calf.

STEP 4: As the ball reaches the back of your knee, quickly but smoothly kick your lower left leg backwards and up, to flick the ball up high! Your left leg will leave the floor and the right foot will come back down to balance you.

STEP 5: As you get better at flicking the ball up, you will begin to get better at controlling the direction it goes in, too.

TEST YOUR KNOWLEDGE

1. What was Alex's nickname at the age of five?

2. Which baseball team did Alex watch with her family when she was little?

3. Who did the United States beat in the 1999 Women's World Cup Final at the Rose Bowl in Pasadena?

4. What was the name of the first football club that Alex joined, located in Orange County, California?

5. What were the names of the two assistant coaches at that club, who gave Alex extra support and training?

6. Which university did Alex gain an athletic scholarship to?

7. What was the name of the California Golden Bears' coach?

8. Which country hosted the U-20 Women's World Cup in 2008?

9. Which country is the United States' former soccer coach Pia Sundhage from?

10. What nickname did the American national team give Alex?

11. For which American football legend does Alex wear the Number 13 shirt?

12. What colour hairband does Alex wear?

13. Who did the United States beat 14–0 in the Olympics 2012 qualifiers?

14. What was the final score in the United States match against Japan in the 2015 Women's World Cup Final?

Answers below. . . No cheating!

1. *Mighty Mouse* 2. *Anaheim Angels* 3. *China* 4. *Cypress Elite*
5. *Sal and Eduardo* 6. *University of California Berkeley (Cal for short)*
7. *Neil McGuire* 8. *Chile* 9. *Sweden* 10. *Baby Horse* 11. *Kristine Lilly*
12. *Pink* 13. *Dominican Republic* 14. *5–2 to the US*

HAVE YOU GOT THEM ALL?

This summer, the world's best footballers will pull on their country's colours to go head to head for the ultimate prize - the FIFA Women's World Cup.

Celebrate by making sure you read the stories of three more Ultimate Football Heroes!

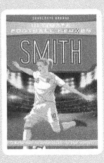